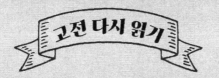

고전 다시 읽기

인형의 집

헨리크 입센 지음

박정미 옮김

희곡
대화체
영한대역

술술
읽히는
영어원서

영어
음성파일
QR코드

인형의 집

발 행 | 2024년 1월 12일
저 자 | 헨리크 입센
옮긴이 | 박정미
펴낸곳 | 제이미북스잉
출판사등록 | 2022.12.12.(제2022-000047호)
주 소 | 서울특별시 도봉구 시루봉로5길48
ISBN | 979-11-984172-4-4(03850)
가 격 | 29,900원
ⓒ 박정미 2024

인형의 집
(A Doll's House)

헨리크 입센 지음
박정미 옮김

CONTENT

순서

DRAMATIS PERSONAE

Torvald Helmer.

Nora, his wife.

Doctor Rank.

Mrs Linde.

Nils Krogstad.

Helmer's three young children.

Anne, their nurse.

Helen, housemaid.

A Porter.

[The action takes place in Helmer's house.]

등장인물

토르발 헬머 노라의 남편

노라 헬머의 아내

랑크 의사이자 토르발의 친구

린데 부인 노라의 친구

크로그스터 변호사

헬머의 세 자녀

안네 헬머 집안의 유모

헬렌 하녀

배달부

(이야기는 헬머 집에서 전개된다.)

ACT I

[SCENE.—A room furnished comfortably and tastefully, but not extravagantly. At the back, a door to the right leads to the entrance-hall, another to the left leads to Helmer's study. Between the doors stands a piano. In the middle of the left-hand wall is a door, and beyond it a window. Near the window are a round table, arm-chairs and a small sofa. In the right-hand wall, at the farther end, another door; and on the same side, nearer the footlights, a stove, two easy chairs and a rocking-chair; between the stove and the door, a small table. Engravings on the walls; a cabinet with china and other small objects; a small book-case with well-bound books. The floors are carpeted, and a fire burns in the stove. It is winter.

A bell rings in the hall; shortly afterwards the door is heard to open. Enter NORA, humming a tune and in high spirits. She is in outdoor dress and carries a number of parcels; these she lays on the table to the right. She leaves the outer door open after her, and through it is seen a PORTER who is carrying a Christmas Tree and a basket, which he gives to the MAID who has opened the door.]

제1막

사치스럽지는 않지만 아늑하고 고상하게 꾸며진 방. 배경으로는, 오른쪽 문이 현관으로 통해있고, 왼쪽 문이 헬머의 서재로 연결된다. 문 사이로 피아노 한 대가 놓여 있다. 왼쪽 벽 가운데에 문이 있고 그 너머에는 창문이 있다. 창가에 둥근 테이블과 안락의자 그리고 작은 소파가 있다. 오른쪽 벽 안쪽에 문이 있고 같은 쪽 무대 가까이에 난로와 안락의자 두 개, 흔들의자 하나가 놓여 있다. 난로와 문 사이에 작은 테이블이 있다. 벽에는 판화가 걸렸고 진열장에는 도자기와 다른 자잘한 물건들이 놓여 있고 양장본 책들이 꽂힌 작은 책장이 있다. 바닥에는 카펫이 깔려 있고 난로에 불이 타고 있다. 어느 겨울날.

현관에서 초인종이 울리고 잠시 후 문이 열리는 소리가 들린다. 콧노래를 하며 활기찬 기운으로 노라가 들어온다. 노라는 외출복을 입고 작은 소포 꾸러미를 들고 있다. 오른쪽 테이블 위에 물건을 올려놓는다. 바깥문을 열어두자, 그 사이로 크리스마스트리와 바구니를 들고 있는 배달부가 보인다. 배달부는 문을 연 하녀에게 물건을 건넨다.

NORA.

Hide the Christmas Tree carefully, Helen. Be sure the children do not see it until this evening, when it is dressed. [To the PORTER, taking out her purse.] How much?

PORTER.

Sixpence.

NORA.

There is a shilling. No, keep the change. [The PORTER thanks her, and goes out. NORA shuts the door. She is laughing to herself, as she takes off her hat and coat. She takes a packet of macaroons from her pocket and eats one or two; then goes cautiously to her husband's door and listens.] Yes, he is in. [Still humming, she goes to the table on the right.]

HELMER.

[calls out from his room]. Is that my little lark twittering out there?

노라

헬렌, 크리스마스트리를 조심히 숨겨줘. 아이들이 오늘 저녁까지 트리를 보지 않도록 해야 해. (배달부에게 가서 지갑을 꺼낸다) 얼마죠?

짐꾼

6펜스입니다.

노라

여기 있어요, 거스름돈은 됐어요. (배달부는 노라에게 감사 인사를 하고 밖으로 나간다. 노라는 문을 닫는다. 자기 모자와 코트를 벗으며 웃는다. 주머니에서 마카롱을 꺼내 한두 개 먹는다. 그리고 남편 방문 쪽으로 살그머니 가서 귀를 댄다) 그이가 안에 있구나. (여전히 콧노래를 하며 오른쪽 테이블로 간다)

헬머

(자신의 방에서 소리친다) 거기 밖에서 지저귀는 건 종달새지?

NORA.

[busy opening some of the parcels]. Yes, it is!

HELMER.

Is it my little squirrel bustling about?

NORA.

Yes!

HELMER.

When did my squirrel come home?

NORA.

Just now. [Puts the bag of macaroons into her pocket and wipes her mouth.] Come in here, Torvald, and see what I have bought.

HELMER.

Don't disturb me. [A little later, he opens the door and looks into the room, pen in hand.] Bought, did you say? All these things? Has my little spendthrift been wasting money again?

노라

(부산스럽게 소포 꾸러미를 열며) 네, 맞아요.

헬머

다람쥐가 돌아다니는 건가?

노라

네!

헬머

다람쥐가 언제 집에 왔지?

노라

방금요. (마카롱 봉지를 주머니 안에 넣고 입을 닦는다) 토르발, 이쪽
으로 와서 제가 산 것 좀 보세요.

헬머

방해하지 마. (잠시 후. 그는 손에 펜을 든 채 문을 열고 방안을 본다)
샀다고? 이걸 다? 낭비꾼이 또 돈을 썼단 말이야?

NORA.

Yes but, Torvald, this year we really can let ourselves go a little. This is the first Christmas that we have not needed to economise.

HELMER.

Still, you know, we can't spend money recklessly.

NORA.

Yes, Torvald, we may be a wee bit more reckless now, mayn't we? Just a tiny wee bit! You are going to have a big salary and earn lots and lots of money.

HELMER.

Yes, after the New Year; but then it will be a whole quarter before the salary is due.

NORA.

Pooh! we can borrow until then.

HELMER.

Nora! [Goes up to her and takes her playfully by the ear.] The same little featherhead!

노라

하지만 토르발, 올해는 우리 여유 좀 가져요. 돈 걱정할 필요 없는 첫 크리스마스잖아요.

헬머

그래도, 우리는 돈을 흥청망청 쓰면 안 되는 걸 알잖아.

노라

토르발, 우리 이제 조금은 더 써도 되잖아요, 그렇죠? 아주 조금만! 당신은 곧 월급을 많이 받고 돈도 많이 벌게 되잖아요.

헬머

내년 후에나 그렇지. 하지만 월급을 받기까지 석 달이나 남았어.

노라

흥! 그럼, 그때까지 빌려 쓸 수 있어요.

헬머

노라! (그녀에게 다가가 장난스럽게 귀를 당긴다) 바보 같기는!

Suppose, now, that I borrowed fifty pounds today, and you spent it all in the Christmas week, and then on New Year's Eve a slate fell on my head and killed me, and—

NORA.

[putting her hands over his mouth]. Oh! don't say such horrid things.

HELMER.

Still, suppose that happened,—what then?

NORA.

If that were to happen, I don't suppose I should care whether I owed money or not.

HELMER.

Yes, but what about the people who had lent it?

NORA.

They? Who would bother about them? I should not know who they were.

자, 생각해 봐. 내가 만약 오늘 50파운드를 빌렸는데 당신이 크리스마스 주에 다 써버리고 새해 전날에 기왓장이 내 머리 위에 떨어져 내가 죽는다면, 그리고…….

노라

(자기 손을 헬머 입술에 대며) 오! 그런 끔찍한 얘기는 하지 말아요.

헬머

그래도 만약 그런 일이 일어난다면 어떻게 하겠어?

노라

만약 그런 일이 일어난다면, 제가 돈을 빚겼든 말든 상관할 바가 아니라고 봐요.

헬머

그렇지만 돈 빌려준 사람들은 어떻게 할까?

노라

빚쟁이들이요? 누가 그들을 신경 쓰죠? 저는 그들이 누군지 알 바 아니에요.

HELMER.

That is like a woman! But seriously, Nora, you know what I think about that. No debt, no borrowing. There can be no freedom or beauty about a home life that depends on borrowing and debt. We two have kept bravely on the straight road so far, and we will go on the same way for the short time longer that there need be any struggle.

NORA.

[moving towards the stove]. As you please, Torvald.

HELMER.

[following her]. Come, come, my little skylark must not droop her wings. What is this! Is my little squirrel out of temper? [Taking out his purse.] Nora, what do you think I have got here?

NORA.

[turning round quickly]. Money!

HELMER.

There you are. [Gives her some money.] Do you think I don't know what a lot is wanted for housekeeping at Christmas-time?

헬머

당신도 다른 여자와 별반 다를 게 없군! 하지만 진지하게 말하지만 내가 그 점에 대해 어떻게 생각하는지 당신도 알고 있어. 절대 빚지지도 말고 돈 빌려서도 안 돼. 돈 빌리거나 빚이 있는 가정은 자유도 없고 멋스러움도 없이 살아가기 마련이야. 오늘날까지 우리는 잘 참고 살아왔어, 그리고 다툼이 있을지라도 조금만 더 참고 계속하던 대로 나아가면 돼.

노라

(난로 쪽으로 가면서) 당신 원하는 대로 하세요, 토르발.

헬머

(노라를 따라가며) 자, 자, 내 작은 종달새 날개가 움츠러들어서는 안 되지. 왜 그래? 귀여운 다람쥐 화났어? (지갑을 꺼내며) 노라, 내가 지금 여기 갖고 있는 게 뭘 것 같아?

노라

(재빠르게 뒤를 돌며) 돈이요!

헬머

여기 봐. (노라에게 돈을 건넨다) 크리스마스 시즌에는 집안에 뭐가 필요한지 내가 모를 것 같아?

NORA.

[counting]. Ten shillings—a pound—two pounds! Thank you, thank you, Torvald; that will keep me going for a long time.

HELMER.

Indeed it must.

NORA.

Yes, yes, it will. But come here and let me show you what I have bought. And all so cheap! Look, here is a new suit for Ivar, and a sword; and a horse and a trumpet for Bob; and a doll and dolly's bedstead for Emmy,—they are very plain, but anyway she will soon break them in pieces. And here are dress-lengths and handkerchiefs for the maids; old Anne ought really to have something better.

HELMER.

And what is in this parcel?

NORA.

[crying out]. No, no! you mustn't see that until this evening.

노라

(돈을 세며) 십 실링, 원 파운드, 투 파운드! 고마워요, 토르발! 당분간 잘 쓸게요.

헬머

당연히 그래야지.

노라

네, 네, 그럴게요. 이쪽으로 와서 제가 뭘 샀는지 보여 드릴게요. 모두 저렴한 것들이에요! 보세요, 이바르 새 옷과 장남감이고 말과 나팔은 보브 것이고 인형과 인형 침대는 에이미 것이에요. 매우 평범하지요. 하지만 어쨌든 그 애는 곧 망가트려요. 그리고 이건 헬렌 옷가지와 손수건이에요. 안네에게 더 좋은 것을 주고 싶네요.

헬머

안에 포장된 것은 뭐야?

노라

(소리 지르며) 안 돼요, 안 돼! 오늘 밤까지 절대 봐서는 안 돼요!

HELMER.

Very well. But now tell me, you extravagant little person, what would you like for yourself?

NORA.

For myself? Oh, I am sure I don't want anything.

HELMER.

Yes, but you must. Tell me something reasonable that you would particularly like to have.

NORA.

No, I really can't think of anything—unless, Torvald—

HELMER.

Well?

NORA.

[playing with his coat buttons, and without raising her eyes to his]. If you really want to give me something, you might—you might—

HELMER.

Well, out with it!

헬머

좋아. 낭비꾼 여사님, 당신 뭐 갖고 싶은 거 있어? 말해 봐.

노라

저요? 저는 아무것도 필요 없어요.

헬머

그래도 뭔가 있겠지, 당신이 정말 갖고 싶은 것으로 뭔가 적당한 게 있으면 말해 봐.

노라

아니에요, 저 정말 아무 생각도 안 나요. 하지만, 여보⋯⋯.

헬머

응?

노라

(남편의 눈을 마주치지 않고 그의 코트 단추를 만지작거린다) **만약 제게 뭔가 주고 싶다면, 그건 바로⋯⋯.**

헬머

말해 봐!

NORA.

[speaking quickly]. You might give me money, Torvald. Only just as much as you can afford; and then one of these days I will buy something with it.

HELMER.

But, Nora—

NORA.

Oh, do! dear Torvald; please, please do! Then I will wrap it up in beautiful gilt paper and hang it on the Christmas Tree. Wouldn't that be fun?

HELMER.

What are little people called that are always wasting money?

NORA.

Spendthrifts—I know. Let us do as I suggest, Torvald, and then I shall have time to think what I am most in want of. That is a very sensible plan, isn't it?

노라

(빠르게 말하며) 돈을 주시면 좋겠어요. 당신이 감당할 수 있을 만큼이면 돼요. 그러면 조만간 그 돈으로 뭔가 살 거예요.

헬머

하지만, 노라 ······.

노라

오, 제발요! 토르발, 그렇게 해주세요! 그러면 그 돈을 예쁜 금종이에 포장해서 크리스마스트리에 달아놓을 거예요. 재밌을 것 같지 않아요?

헬머

돈을 늘 낭비하는 귀여운 사람을 뭐라고 부르지?

노라

낭비꾼들. 저도 알아요. 제 말대로 해주세요, 토르발. 그러면 무엇이 가장 필요한지 생각할게요. 꽤 합리적인 계획 아닌가요?

HELMER.

[smiling]. Indeed it is—that is to say, if you were really to save out of the money I give you, and then really buy something for yourself. But if you spend it all on the housekeeping and any number of unnecessary things, then I merely have to pay up again.

NORA.

Oh but, Torvald—

HELMER.

You can't deny it, my dear little Nora. [Puts his arm round her waist.] It's a sweet little spendthrift, but she uses up a deal of money. One would hardly believe how expensive such little persons are!

NORA.

It's a shame to say that. I do really save all I can.

HELMER.

[laughing]. That's very true,—all you can. But you can't save anything!

NORA.

[smiling quietly and happily]. You haven't any idea how many expenses we skylarks and squirrels have, Torvald.

헬머

(미소 지으며) 그렇긴 해. 말하자면 내가 주는 돈을 정말로 저축하고 당신을 위해 뭔가를 산다면 말이야. 하지만 당신이 만약 집안일과 쓸데없는 것들에 전부 돈을 쓴다면 나는 또다시 지불해야 해.

노라

하지만, 여보…….

헬머

내 귀여운 노라, 부정할 수 없지. (노라 허리를 팔로 두른다) 예쁜 낭비꾼은 돈을 많이 쓴단 말이야. 이런 사람들이 얼마나 비싼지 누가 믿을 수 있을까!

노라

그렇게 말씀하시니 섭섭해요. 저는 정말 가능한 한 절약하고 있는데요.

헬머

(웃으며) 그래 맞아. 당신 기준에서는 그렇지. 하지만 전혀 아무것도 아끼지 않아.

노라

(조용히 그리고 행복하게 미소 지으며) 당신은 우리 종달새나 다람쥐에게 돈이 얼마나 많이 드는지 몰라요, 토르발.

HELMER.

You are an odd little soul. Very like your father. You always find some new way of wheedling money out of me, and, as soon as you have got it, it seems to melt in your hands. You never know where it has gone. Still, one must take you as you are. It is in the blood; for indeed it is true that you can inherit these things, Nora.

NORA.

Ah, I wish I had inherited many of papa's qualities.

HELMER.

And I would not wish you to be anything but just what you are, my sweet little skylark. But, do you know, it strikes me that you are looking rather—what shall I say—rather uneasy today?

NORA.

Do I?

HELMER.

You do, really. Look straight at me.

헬머

당신은 참 묘해. 장인어른과 매우 닮았지. 나를 구슬려 돈을 가져가는 새로운 방법을 늘 찾고 돈을 손에 쥐자마자 사라지는 것 같아. 당신은 돈이 어디로 갔는지 절대 모르고 말이야. 그래도 당신을 있는 그대로 받아들여야 하지. 이건 집안 내력이야. 실제로 당신이 이러한 것들을 물려받은 것은 사실이야, 노라.

노라

아, 아버지의 성품을 많이 이어받았더라면 좋았겠어요.

헬머

난 당신 자신이 아닌 누군가가 되는 것을 바라지 않아. 내 사랑스러운 종달새. 그런데, 뭐랄까. 당신 오늘 좀 불안해 보인다는 생각이 드는데?

노라

제가요?

헬머

응, 정말 그래. 나를 똑바로 봐.

NORA.

[looks at him]. Well?

HELMER.

[wagging his finger at her]. Hasn't Miss Sweet Tooth been breaking rules in town today?

NORA.

No; what makes you think that?

HELMER.

Hasn't she paid a visit to the confectioner's?

NORA.

No, I assure you, Torvald—

HELMER.

Not been nibbling sweets?

NORA.

No, certainly not.

노라

(남편을 본다) 됐어요?

헬머

(그녀에게 손가락을 까딱거리며) 오늘 참새가 방앗간에 들린 것 같은
데?

노라

아니에요, 왜 그렇게 생각해요?

헬머

제과점에 들르지 않았어?

노라

아니라니까요, 토르발.

헬머

단 거 한두 개 먹지 않았어?

노라

정말 아니에요.

HELMER.

Not even taken a bite at a macaroon or two?

NORA.

No, Torvald, I assure you really—

HELMER.

There, there, of course I was only joking.

NORA.

[going to the table on the right]. I should not think of going against your wishes.

HELMER.

No, I am sure of that; besides, you gave me your word — [Going up to her.] Keep your little Christmas secrets to yourself, my darling. They will all be revealed tonight when the Christmas Tree is lit, no doubt.

NORA.

Did you remember to invite Doctor Rank?

헬머

마카롱 한두 개도 먹지 않았어?

노라

아니에요, 토르발, 저 정말로 장담해요.

헬머

됐어, 됐어, 농담이었어.

노라

(오른쪽 테이블로 간다) 당신 뜻에 반하는 것은 생각하지도 않아요.

헬머

그래, 그건 확실하지. 게다가 당신이 내게 약속했고 말이야. (노라 쪽으로 간다) 내 사랑, 당신의 소중한 크리스마스 비밀은 혼자 간직해. 오늘 밤 크리스마스트리에 불이 켜지면 모두 드러나게 될 것이지만 말이야.

노라

랑크 선생님 초대하는 거 잊지 않았죠?

HELMER.

No. But there is no need; as a matter of course he will come to dinner with us. However, I will ask him when he comes in this morning. I have ordered some good wine. Nora, you can't think how I am looking forward to this evening.

NORA.

So am I! And how the children will enjoy themselves, Torvald!

HELMER.

It is splendid to feel that one has a perfectly safe appointment, and a big enough income. It's delightful to think of, isn't it?

NORA.

It's wonderful!

HELMER.

Do you remember last Christmas? For a full three weeks beforehand you shut yourself up every evening until long after midnight, making ornaments for the Christmas Tree, and all the other fine things that were to be a surprise to us. It was the dullest three weeks I ever spent!

헬머

아니, 그럴 필요 없어. 랑크 선생이 와서 우리와 함께 저녁 식사 하는 것은 늘 있는 일이니까. 그렇지만 오늘 아침에 그가 오면 얘기해야지. 고급 와인도 주문했어. 노라, 내가 오늘 밤을 얼마나 기대하는지 당신은 알지 못할 거야.

노라

저도 그래요. 애들도 즐거워할 거예요. 토르발!

헬머

지극히 안정적인 지위에 두둑한 수입까지 생기니 정말 멋진 일이야. 생각만으로도 기쁘지 않아?

노라

정말 대단해요!

헬머

당신 지난 크리스마스 기억나? 삼 주 동안 당신은 매일 밤늦게까지 틀어박혀서 크리스마스트리 장식과 우리를 놀라게 하려고 다른 좋은 것들을 만들었지. 가장 지루하게 보낸 삼 주였어.

NORA.

I didn't find it dull.

HELMER.

[smiling]. But there was precious little result, Nora.

NORA.

Oh, you shouldn't tease me about that again. How could I help the cat's going in and tearing everything to pieces?

HELMER.

Of course you couldn't, poor little girl. You had the best of intentions to please us all, and that's the main thing. But it is a good thing that our hard times are over.

NORA.

Yes, it is really wonderful.

HELMER.

This time I needn't sit here and be dull all alone, and you needn't ruin your dear eyes and your pretty little hands—

노라

저는 지루하지 않았어요.

헬머

(미소 지으며) 하지만 결과가 별로 좋지 않았어, 노라.

노라

어머, 그 일로 저를 놀리지 마세요. 고양이가 들어와서 모두 갈기갈기 찢어놓은 것을 제가 어떻게 할 수 있었겠어요?

헬머

당연히 당신이 어쩔 수 없었지. 우리 모두를 기쁘게 해주려는 좋은 의도로 그랬으니까, 그게 중요해. 괴로운 시간이 지나서 다행이야.

노라

맞아요, 정말 다행이에요.

헬머

나도 여기에 앉아서 홀로 지루하게 지낼 필요도 없고 당신도 예쁜 눈과 작고 귀여운 손을 혹사할 필요가 없어.

NORA.

[clapping her hands]. No, Torvald, I needn't any longer, need I! It's wonderfully lovely to hear you say so! [Taking his arm.] Now I will tell you how I have been thinking we ought to arrange things, Torvald. As soon as Christmas is over—[A bell rings in the hall.] There's the bell. [She tidies the room a little.] There's some one at the door. What a nuisance!

HELMER.

If it is a caller, remember I am not at home.

MAID.

[in the doorway]. A lady to see you, ma'am,—a stranger.

NORA.

Ask her to come in.

MAID.

[to HELMER]. The doctor came at the same time, sir.

노라

(손뼉을 친다) 맞아요, 토르발, 저는 더 이상 그럴 필요가 없어요. 당신이 하는 말을 들으니 정말 기쁘네요! (남편의 팔을 잡는다) 우리가 어떻게 일을 처리해야 할지 제가 생각한 것을 이제 말씀드릴게요. 크리스마스가 끝나자마자 …… (현관에서 초인종이 울린다) 초인종이 울리네요. (방 안을 조금 치운다) 누가 왔어요. 아휴 귀찮아!

헬머

손님이라면, 나는 집에 없는 사람이야.

하녀

(출입구에서) 마님, 어떤 여자분이 찾아오셨어요.

노라

들어오시게 해.

하녀

(헬머에게) 의사 선생님도 오셨어요.

HELMER.

Did he go straight into my room?

MAID.

Yes, sir.

[HELMER goes into his room. The MAID ushers in Mrs Linde, who is in travelling dress, and shuts the door.]

MRS LINDE.

[in a dejected and timid voice]. How do you do, Nora?

NORA.

[doubtfully]. How do you do—

MRS LINDE.

You don't recognise me, I suppose.

NORA.

No, I don't know—yes, to be sure, I seem to— [Suddenly.] Yes! Christine! Is it really you?

MRS LINDE.

Yes, it is I.

헬머

내 방으로 바로 들어가셨지?

하녀

네, 나리.

(헬머는 자신의 방으로 들어간다. 하녀는 여행복 차림의 린데 부인을 안내하고 문을 닫는다)

린데 부인

(기운 없고 소심한 목소리로) 노라, 잘 지냈니?

노라

(의심스럽게) 안녕하세요…….

린데 부인

나를 못 알아보는구나.

노라

네, 모르겠어요…… 확실히, 제가 보기엔…… (갑자기) 아! 크리스티네! 정말 너니?

린데 부인

그래, 나야.

NORA.

Christine! To think of my not recognising you! And yet how could I—[In a gentle voice.] How you have altered, Christine!

MRS LINDE.

Yes, I have indeed. In nine, ten long years—

NORA.

Is it so long since we met? I suppose it is. The last eight years have been a happy time for me, I can tell you. And so now you have come into the town, and have taken this long journey in winter—that was plucky of you.

MRS LINDE.

I arrived by steamer this morning.

NORA.

To have some fun at Christmas-time, of course. How delightful! We will have such fun together! But take off your things. You are not cold, I hope. [Helps her.] Now we will sit down by the stove, and be cosy.

노라

크리스티네! 너를 몰라보다니⋯⋯. (조용한 소리로) 달라졌구나, 크리스티네.

린데 부인

응, 그렇지. 9년, 10년이 흘렀으니⋯⋯.

노라

우리가 만난 지가 그렇게 오래되었나? 그런 것 같네. 지난 8년 동안 난 행복한 시간을 보냈어. 정말이야. 이제 이 지역에 왔구나, 한겨울에 긴 여행을 하다니, 용감하구나.

린데 부인

오늘 아침 증기선으로 도착했어.

노라

물론 크리스마스를 즐겁게 보내기 위해서겠지. 정말 기뻐! 우리 함께 즐겁게 지내자! 외투 벗어. 네가 춥지 않았으면 좋겠어. (린데 부인을 돕는다) 난로 옆에 앉아서 편히 쉬어.

No, take this armchair; I will sit here in the rocking-chair. [Takes her hands.] Now you look like your old self again; it was only the first moment—You are a little paler, Christine, and perhaps a little thinner.

MRS LINDE.

And much, much older, Nora.

NORA.

Perhaps a little older; very, very little; certainly not much. [Stops suddenly and speaks seriously.] What a thoughtless creature I am, chattering away like this. My poor, dear Christine, do forgive me.

MRS LINDE.

What do you mean, Nora?

NORA.

[gently]. Poor Christine, you are a widow.

MRS LINDE.

Yes; it is three years ago now.

아니, 여기 안락의자에 앉아. 나는 흔들의자 앉을게. (린데 부인의 손을 잡는다) 이제 보니 예전 모습 같아. 처음 봤을 때는 못 알아봤어 …… 크리스티네, 약간 창백하고 조금 야윈 것 같아.

린데 부인

많이 늙었지, 노라.

노라

약간 그렇지만 아주 조금. 많이는 아니야. (갑자기 말을 중단하고 진지하게 말한다) 왜 이렇게 생각이 없을까, 이렇게 수다만 떨고 있으니! 가여운 크리스티네, 미안해.

린데 부인

무슨 말이야, 노라?

노라

(조용히) 불쌍한 크리스티네, 미망인이 되었다면서.

린데 부인

그래, 삼 년 전이지.

NORA.

Yes, I knew; I saw it in the papers. I assure you, Christine, I meant ever so often to write to you at the time, but I always put it off and something always prevented me.

MRS LINDE.

I quite understand, dear.

NORA.

It was very bad of me, Christine. Poor thing, how you must have suffered. And he left you nothing?

MRS LINDE.

No.

NORA.

And no children?

MRS LINDE.

No.

NORA.

Nothing at all, then.

노라

신문 보고 알았어. 그때 몇 번이나 편지를 쓰려고 했는데 자꾸 일이 생기는 바람에 항상 미뤘어. 크리스티네, 정말이야.

린데 부인

충분히 이해해.

노라

내가 정말 나빴어. 가여운 크리스티네, 얼마나 힘들었겠어. 그리고 남편이 남겨준 것은 없었니?

린데 부인

없어.

노라

그러면 아이는 없어?

린데 부인

없어.

로라

그럼, 아무것도 없구나.

MRS LINDE.

Not even any sorrow or grief to live upon.

NORA.

[looking incredulously at her]. But, Christine, is that possible?

MRS LINDE.

[smiles sadly and strokes her hair]. It sometimes happens, Nora.

NORA.

So you are quite alone. How dreadfully sad that must be. I have three lovely children. You can't see them just now, for they are out with their nurse. But now you must tell me all about it.

MRS LINDE.

No, no; I want to hear about you.

NORA.

No, you must begin. I mustn't be selfish today; today I must only think of your affairs. But there is one thing I must tell you. Do you know we have just had a great piece of good luck?

린데 부인

살아가는데 어떤 슬픔과 고통조차 없어.

노라

(믿기지 않는다는 듯이 린데 부인을 보며) 하지만 크리스티네, 어쩜 그럴 수가 있니?

린데 보인

(슬프게 미소 짓고 머리를 쓰다듬는다) 때로는 그런 일도 일어나지, 노라.

노라

그러면 완전히 혼자구나. 얼마나 몹시 슬프겠어. 난 사랑스러운 세 아이가 있어. 유모가 아이들을 데리고 나가서 지금은 볼 수가 없어. 암튼 네 얘기 좀 들려줘.

린데 부인

아니, 난 네 얘기를 듣고 싶어.

노라

아니야, 네가 먼저 해. 오늘 내 생각만 하지 않고 네 일만 생각할래. 그런데 한 가지 말해야 할 게 있어. 최근에 우리가 굉장한 행운을 얻었다는 거 알고 있니?

MRS LINDE.

No, what is it?

NORA.

Just fancy, my husband has been made manager of the Bank!

MRS LINDE.

Your husband? What good luck!

NORA.

Yes, tremendous! A barrister's profession is such an uncertain thing, especially if he won't undertake unsavoury cases; and naturally Torvald has never been willing to do that, and I quite agree with him. You may imagine how pleased we are! He is to take up his work in the Bank at the New Year, and then he will have a big salary and lots of commissions. For the future we can live quite differently—we can do just as we like. I feel so relieved and so happy, Christine! It will be splendid to have heaps of money and not need to have any anxiety, won't it?

린데 부인

아니, 무슨 일인데?

노라

글쎄 말이야, 남편이 은행장이 됐어!

린데 부인

네 남편이? 정말 좋은 일이네!

노라

그래, 대단하지! 변호사 직업은 불안정한데 특히나 그이가 불미스러운 사건은 맡지 않으려고 하니까. 물론 토르발이 그런 일을 하려고 한 적도 없고 그 점은 나도 찬성이야. 그러니 우리가 얼마나 기쁘겠니! 새해에는 남편이 은행에서 일을 하고, 많은 급여와 수수료를 받을 거야. 앞으로는 다르게 살 수 있어. 우리가 하고 싶은 대로 말이야. 난 정말 편안하고 행복해, 크리스티네! 경제적으로 넉넉해서 더 이상 걱정 안 해도 되니 얼마나 좋은 일이야, 그렇지 않니?

MRS LINDE.

Yes, anyhow I think it would be delightful to have what one needs.

NORA.

No, not only what one needs, but heaps and heaps of money.

MRS LINDE.

[smiling]. Nora, Nora, haven't you learned sense yet? In our schooldays you were a great spendthrift.

NORA.

[laughing]. Yes, that is what Torvald says now. [Wags her finger at her.] But "Nora, Nora" is not so silly as you think. We have not been in a position for me to waste money. We have both had to work.

MRS LINDE.

You too?

린데 부인

그렇지, 어쨌든 필요한 것을 가질 수 있다는 건 정말 좋은 일이라고 생각해.

노라

아니, 필요한 것뿐만 아니라 아주 많은 돈이야.

린데 부인

(미소 지으며) 노라, 넌 아직도 정신 못 차렸니? 학창 시절에도 낭비가 심했는데.

노라

(웃으며) 응, 토르발은 지금도 그렇게 말해. (손가락을 까닥거린다) 하지만 "노라, 노라"는 네가 생각하는 것만큼 어리석지 않아. 우리 상황에 내가 돈을 낭비할 정도는 아니야. 우린 둘 다 일해야만 하지.

린데 부인

너도 말이야?

NORA.

Yes; odds and ends, needlework, crotchet-work, embroidery, and that kind of thing. [Dropping her voice.] And other things as well. You know Torvald left his office when we were married? There was no prospect of promotion there, and he had to try and earn more than before. But during the first year he over-worked himself dreadfully. You see, he had to make money every way he could, and he worked early and late; but he couldn't stand it, and fell dreadfully ill, and the doctors said it was necessary for him to go south.

MRS LINDE.

You spent a whole year in Italy, didn't you?

NORA.

Yes. It was no easy matter to get away, I can tell you. It was just after Ivar was born; but naturally we had to go. It was a wonderfully beautiful journey, and it saved Torvald's life. But it cost a tremendous lot of money, Christine.

MRS LINDE.

So I should think.

노라

응, 자질구레한 일들이지, 바느질, 뜨개질, 자수, 뭐 이런 일들. (목소리를 낮춘다) 그리고 다른 것도 해. 우리가 결혼할 때 토르발이 퇴사한 거 알지? 거기서 승진할 가능성도 없었고 남편은 그전보다 더 많이 벌어야만 했어. 그런데 처음 일 년 동안 너무 무리하게 일했지 뭐야. 할 수 있는 모든 방법으로 돈을 벌어야 했고 아침부터 저녁까지 일했지. 하지만 견디지 못해 지독한 병에 걸렸고 의사가 말하길 남편은 반드시 남쪽으로 요양 가야 한다고 하더라고.

린데부인

일 년 동안 이탈리아에서 지낸 거였니?

노라

맞아. 떠난다는 것이 쉬운 일은 아니었어, 이바르가 태어난 직후였거든. 하지만 우리는 당연히 가야만 했어. 아주 멋지고 아름다운 여행이었고 덕분에 토르발 목숨도 살릴 수 있었어. 하지만 돈이 엄청 많이 들었지, 크리스티네.

린데

그랬겠네.

NORA.

It cost about two hundred and fifty pounds. That's a lot, isn't it?

MRS LINDE.

Yes, and in emergencies like that it is lucky to have the money.

NORA.

I ought to tell you that we had it from papa.

MRS LINDE.

Oh, I see. It was just about that time that he died, wasn't it?

NORA.

Yes; and, just think of it, I couldn't go and nurse him. I was expecting little Ivar's birth every day and I had my poor sick Torvald to look after. My dear, kind father—I never saw him again, Christine. That was the saddest time I have known since our marriage.

노라

약 250파운드 정도 들었어. 정말 큰돈이지?

린데 부인

그래, 그래도 위급할 때 그만한 돈이 있어서 다행이야.

노라

그 돈은 아버지께 빌린 돈이었어.

린데 부인

오, 그리고 보니 그 무렵에 아버님이 돌아가셨지, 그렇지?

노라

맞아. 생각해 봐, 난 아버지께 가서 간호할 수 없었어. 이바르 출산일이 다가왔고 아픈 토르발도 보살펴야 했지. 사랑하는 다정하신 아버지를 이제 다시 볼 수 없었어, 크리스티네. 그때가 결혼 이후 가장 슬픈 시간이었어.

MRS LINDE.

I know how fond you were of him. And then you went off to Italy?

NORA.

Yes; you see we had money then, and the doctors insisted on our going, so we started a month later.

MRS LINDE.

And your husband came back quite well?

NORA.

As sound as a bell!

MRS LINDE.

But—the doctor?

NORA.

What doctor?

MRS LINDE.

I thought your maid said the gentleman who arrived here just as I did, was the doctor?

린데 부인

네가 아버지를 얼마나 좋아했는지 알지. 그럼, 그때 이탈리아로 떠났니?

노라

응, 우린 돈도 마련되었고 의사가 요양 가야 한다고 재촉하니 그래서 한 달 후에 떠났어.

린데 부인

남편은 완전히 회복되어 돌아온 거야?

노라

아주 건강해졌어!

린데 부인

그런데 그 의사 선생님은?

노라

어떤 의사 선생님?

린데 부인

내가 들어올 때 여기에 막 도착하신 신사분이 의사 선생님이라고 하녀가 말한 것 같던데.

NORA.

Yes, that was Doctor Rank, but he doesn't come here professionally. He is our greatest friend, and comes in at least once every day. No, Torvald has not had an hour's illness since then, and our children are strong and healthy and so am I. [Jumps up and claps her hands.] Christine! Christine! it's good to be alive and happy!—But how horrid of me; I am talking of nothing but my own affairs. [Sits on a stool near her, and rests her arms on her knees.] You mustn't be angry with me. Tell me, is it really true that you did not love your husband? Why did you marry him?

MRS LINDE.

My mother was alive then, and was bedridden and helpless, and I had to provide for my two younger brothers; so I did not think I was justified in refusing his offer.

NORA.

No, perhaps you were quite right. He was rich at that time, then?

노라

아, 그분은 랑크 의사 선생님이셔. 그런데 여기에 업무상 온 것이 아니고. 우리와 친한 분이라 매일 한 번은 오시지. 토르발은 그때 이후 병에 걸리지 않았고 우리 아이들도 매우 건강하고 나도 역시 그렇지. (벌떡 일어서며 손뼉을 친다) 크리스티네! 크리스티네! 살아있고 행복해서 너무 좋아! 내 정신 좀 봐, 너무 내 얘기만 했네. (린데 부인 가까이에 있는 걸상에 앉으며 두 손을 그녀의 무릎 위에 얹고) 언짢게 생각하지 말고, 말해 봐. 남편을 사랑하지 않았다는 것이 사실이니? 왜 그 사람과 결혼했어?

린데 부인

그때 어머니가 살아계셨고, 몸져누워 계셔서 스스로를 돌보실 수 없었어. 게다가 어린 두 동생을 부양해야만 했지. 그래서 그의 청혼을 거절하는 것이 옳다고 생각하지 않았어.

노라

그래, 아마도 네가 아주 옳았는지도 몰라. 남편은 그 당시 부자였니?

MRS LINDE.

I believe he was quite well off. But his business was a precarious one; and, when he died, it all went to pieces and there was nothing left.

NORA.

And then?—

MRS LINDE.

Well, I had to turn my hand to anything I could find— first a small shop, then a small school, and so on. The last three years have seemed like one long working-day, with no rest. Now it is at an end, Nora. My poor mother needs me no more, for she is gone; and the boys do not need me either; they have got situations and can shift for themselves.

NORA.

What a relief you must feel if—

MRS LINDE.

No, indeed; I only feel my life unspeakably empty. No one to live for anymore. [Gets up restlessly.]

린데 부인

꽤 잘 살았던 것 같아. 하지만 남편 사업은 불안정했어. 그가 세상을 뜨자, 모든 것이 무너졌고 남은 것은 없었지.

노라

그런 다음에는?

린데 부인

내가 찾을 수 있는 어떤 일이든 시작했어, 처음에는 작은 가게도 해보고 다음에는 조그마한 학원도 하고 뭐 이것저것. 지난 삼 년은 쉴 틈 없이 오래 일하는 하루 같았어. 하지만 그것도 끝났어, 노라. 불쌍한 어머니가 더 이상 나를 찾지 않으시지, 왜냐하면 돌아가셨거든. 동생들도 마찬가지야. 모두 직장을 잡고 각자 자립해서 살고 있거든.

노라

이젠 안심이 되겠구나.

린데 부인

아니, 사실 난 말할 수 없는 공허감을 느낄 뿐이야. 더 이상 살아갈 동기가 없어. (불안하게 일어선다)

That was why I could not stand the life in my little backwater any longer. I hope it may be easier here to find something which will busy me and occupy my thoughts. If only I could have the good luck to get some regular work—office work of some kind—

NORA.

But, Christine, that is so frightfully tiring, and you look tired out now. You had far better go away to some watering-place.

MRS LINDE.

[walking to the window]. I have no father to give me money for a journey, Nora.

NORA.

[rising]. Oh, don't be angry with me!

MRS LINDE.

[going up to her]. It is you that must not be angry with me, dear. The worst of a position like mine is that it makes one so bitter. No one to work for, and yet obliged to be always on the lookout for chances.

그래서 이제 더 이상 후미진 곳에서 살아갈 수 없었어. 분주하고 마음을 다잡을 뭔가를 여기서 쉽게 찾을 수 있을 거라고 기대하고 있어. 사무직 같은 상근직을 운 좋게 얻을 수 있다면 좋겠어.

노라

하지만 크리스티네, 그런 일은 무척 힘들어. 그리고 너는 지금 매우 지쳐 보여. 온천 같은데 쉬러 가는 게 훨씬 나을 텐데.

린데 부인

(창가로 간다) 여행 경비를 대줄 아버지도 없어, 노라.

노라

(일어서며) 기분 나쁘게 생각하지 말아줘!

린데 부인

(노라에게 간다). 너야말로 나 때문에 기분 나쁘게 생각하지 마! 나 같은 상황에 있는 사람에게 가장 나쁜 건 마음이 비뚤어지는 거란다. 일할 동기는 없지만 그래도 늘 기회를 찾으려고 하지.

One must live, and so one becomes selfish. When you told me of the happy turn your fortunes have taken—you will hardly believe it—I was delighted not so much on your account as on my own.

NORA.

How do you mean?—Oh, I understand. You mean that perhaps Torvald could get you something to do.

MRS LINDE.

Yes, that was what I was thinking of.

NORA.

He must, Christine. Just leave it to me; I will broach the subject very cleverly—I will think of something that will please him very much. It will make me so happy to be of some use to you.

MRS LINDE.

How kind you are, Nora, to be so anxious to help me! It is doubly kind in you, for you know so little of the burdens and troubles of life.

살아야 하니까 이기적으로 되는 거야. 네가 좋은 일이 생겼다고 내게 말했을 때도 믿기 어렵겠지만, 너보다 오히려 내 입장 때문에 더 기뻤어.

노라

무슨 뜻이야? 아, 알겠다. 토르발이 너에게 뭔가 할 수 있는 일이 있다고 생각한 거지.

린데 부인

그래, 그렇게 생각했어.

노라

반드시 해줄 거야, 크리스티네. 내게 맡겨. 내가 그 일에 대해 말을 잘해볼게. 그이를 매우 기쁘게 해줄 뭔가를 생각해서 말이야. 너에게 도움이 된다면 정말 기쁠 거야.

린데 부인

나를 도우려고 이렇게 애써주다니 정말 고마워. 세상 풍파를 모르는 네가 도와주겠다니 더욱 고맙다.

NORA.

I—? I know so little of them?

MRS LINDE.

[smiling]. My dear! Small household cares and that sort of thing!—You are a child, Nora.

NORA.

[tosses her head and crosses the stage]. You ought not to be so superior.

MRS LINDE.

No?

NORA.

You are just like the others. They all think that I am incapable of anything really serious—

MRS LINDE.

Come, come—

NORA.

—that I have gone through nothing in this world of cares.

노라

세상 풍파를 모른다고? 내가?

린데 부인

(미소 지으며) 아이고! 조그마한 집안일이나 뭐 그 정도의 일을 하니까! 너는 아이 같아, 노라.

노라

(머리를 홱 치켜들며 가로질러 간다) 네가 인생 선배라도 된 듯이 굴지 마.

린데 부인

응?

노라

너도 다른 사람과 똑같아. 모두 내가 어떤 진지한 일을 할 수 없다고 생각하거든.

린데 부인

아니, 저기…….

노라

사람들은 내가 고생을 겪어보지 않았다고 생각하지.

MRS LINDE.

But, my dear Nora, you have just told me all your troubles.

NORA.

Pooh!—those were trifles. [Lowering her voice.] I have not told you the important thing.

MRS LINDE.

The important thing? What do you mean?

NORA.

You look down upon me altogether, Christine—but you ought not to. You are proud, aren't you, of having worked so hard and so long for your mother?

MRS LINDE.

Indeed, I don't look down on anyone. But it is true that I am both proud and glad to think that I was privileged to make the end of my mother's life almost free from care.

린데 부인

하지만 노라, 방금 내게 고생한 이야기를 했잖아.

노라

흥! 그건 사소한 거야. (목소리를 낮춘다) 아주 중요한 일은 말하지 않았어.

린데 부인

중요한 일? 무슨 말이니?

노라

너는 나를 얕잡아보고 있어, 크리스티네. 그렇게 보면 안 돼. 넌네 어머니를 위해 힘들게 오랫동안 일한 것을 자랑스러워하지, 그렇지 않니?

린데 부인

정말, 난 누구도 얕잡아 보지 않아. 하지만 어머니의 노후를 위해 걱정시켜 드리지 않게 한 것을 생각하면 나 자신이 뿌듯하고 기쁜 것은 사실이야.

NORA.

And you are proud to think of what you have done for your brothers?

MRS LINDE.

I think I have the right to be.

NORA.

I think so, too. But now, listen to this; I too have something to be proud and glad of.

MRS LINDE.

I have no doubt you have. But what do you refer to?

NORA.

Speak low. Suppose Torvald were to hear! He mustn't on any account—no one in the world must know, Christine, except you.

MRS LINDE.

But what is it?

노라

그리고 동생들을 돌봐준 것도 자랑스럽게 생각하지?

린데 부인

그럴 만하다고 생각해.

노라

나도 그렇게 생각해. 하지만 지금 이 얘기를 들어봐. 나 또한 자랑스럽고 기쁜 일이 있다는 거야.

린데 부인

물론 있겠지. 그런데 무슨 일인데 그래?

노라

목소리 낮춰. 토르발이 들을지도 몰라. 어떤 일이 있어도 남편이 알면 안 돼. 크리스티네, 너 말고는 아무도 알아서는 안 돼.

린데 부인

도대체 무슨 일이야?

NORA.

Come here. [Pulls her down on the sofa beside her.] Now I will show you that I too have something to be proud and glad of. It was I who saved Torvald's life.

MRS LINDE.

"Saved"? How?

NORA.

I told you about our trip to Italy. Torvald would never have recovered if he had not gone there—

MRS LINDE.

Yes, but your father gave you the necessary funds.

NORA.

[smiling]. Yes, that is what Torvald and all the others think, but—

MRS LINDE.

But—

노라

이쪽으로 와 봐. (자신 옆 소파로 린데 부인을 끌어 앉힌다) 내가 자랑스럽고 기쁘게 여기는 일을 알려줄게. 토르발의 목숨을 구한 것은 바로 나였어.

린데 부인

"목숨을 구했다고?" 어떻게?

노라

이탈리아로 여행한 거 얘기했잖아. 만약 토르발이 가지 않았다면 절대 회복하지 못했을 거야.

린데 부인

그렇겠지, 하지만 네 아버님이 자금을 대주셨잖아.

노라

(미소 지으며) 그래, 토르발과 다른 사람들 모두 그렇게 알고 있어, 그런데…….

린데 부인

그런데?

NORA.

Papa didn't give us a shilling. It was I who procured the money.

MRS LINDE.

You? All that large sum?

NORA.

Two hundred and fifty pounds. What do you think of that?

MRS LINDE.

But, Nora, how could you possibly do it? Did you win a prize in the Lottery?

NORA.

[contemptuously]. In the Lottery? There would have been no credit in that.

MRS LINDE.

But where did you get it from, then?

노라

아버지는 한 푼도 주지 않았어. 돈을 마련한 사람은 바로 나야.

린데 부인

네가? 그 큰돈을?

노라

250파운드야. 어떻게 생각해?

린데 부인

하지만 노라, 그걸 어떻게 할 수 있지? 복권에 당첨되기라도 한 거야?

노라

(경멸하듯이) 복권? 그런 건 자랑거리가 아니지.

린데 부인

그러면 어떻게 돈을 구한 거야?

Nora.

[humming and smiling with an air of mystery]. Hm, hm!
Aha!

MRS LINDE.

Because you couldn't have borrowed it.

NORA.

Couldn't I? Why not?

MRS LINDE.

No, a wife cannot borrow without her husband's
consent.

NORA.

[tossing her head]. Oh, if it is a wife who has any head
for business—a wife who has the wit to be a little bit
clever—

MRS LINDE.

I don't understand it at all, Nora.

노라

(흥얼거리며 묘하게 미소 짓는다) 흠, 흠! 하하!

린데 부인

대출이 안 됐을 텐데.

노라

내가 대출이 안 됐을 거라고? 왜 안 되는데?

린데 부인

아니 그게, 주부는 남편 동의 없이 돈 못 빌리잖아.

노라

(머리를 홱 치켜들며) 만약 부인이 사업수완이 있고 현명한 지혜를 가진 아내라면?

린데 부인

무슨 말인지 통 모르겠어, 노라.

NORA.

There is no need you should. I never said I had borrowed the money. I may have got it some other way. [Lies back on the sofa.] Perhaps I got it from some other admirer. When anyone is as attractive as I am—

MRS LINDE.

You are a mad creature.

NORA.

Now, you know you're full of curiosity, Christine.

MRS LINDE.

Listen to me, Nora dear. Haven't you been a little bit imprudent?

NORA.

[sits up straight]. Is it imprudent to save your husband's life?

노라

네가 알 필요 없어. 돈을 빌렸다는 말은 절대 하지 않았어. 다른 방법으로 구했을지도 모르지. (소파에 등을 기대며 눕는다) 아마도 나를 좋아하는 누군가에게 받았을 수도 있잖아. 나처럼 매력적이라면 누군가 ……

린데 부인

미쳤군.

노라

이제, 궁금해서 미치겠지? 크리스티네.

린데 부인

나 좀 봐, 노라. 무슨 경솔한 행동을 한 건 아니지?

노라

(똑바로 앉으며) 남편 목숨을 구하는 일이 경솔한 일이니?

MRS LINDE.

It seems to me imprudent, without his knowledge, to—

NORA.

But it was absolutely necessary that he should not know! My goodness, can't you understand that? It was necessary he should have no idea what a dangerous condition he was in. It was to me that the doctors came and said that his life was in danger, and that the only thing to save him was to live in the south.

Do you suppose I didn't try, first of all, to get what I wanted as if it were for myself? I told him how much I should love to travel abroad like other young wives; I tried tears and entreaties with him; I told him that he ought to remember the condition I was in, and that he ought to be kind and indulgent to me; I even hinted that he might raise a loan. That nearly made him angry, Christine. He said I was thoughtless, and that it was his duty as my husband not to indulge me in my whims and caprices—as I believe he called them. Very well, I thought, you must be saved—and that was how I came to devise a way out of the difficulty—

린데 부인

남편에게 알리지 않고 그런 일을 하는 건 경솔한 것 같아.

노라

하지만 그이가 절대 알아서는 안 됐어! 세상에, 그것도 이해 못하니? 그이는 자신이 위험한 상태라는 것을 알아서는 안 되었어. 의사들이 내게 와서 말하기를 '남편이 위독하다, 남편을 살리려면 남쪽에서 살아야 한다'라고 했지. 우선, 나 자신을 위한 것처럼 원하는 것을 얻기 위해 내가 노력하지 않았다고 생각하니?

다른 젊은 아내들처럼 내가 해외여행을 얼마나 좋아하는지 그이에게 말했어. 정말 눈물로 호소했어, 그리고 내가 어떤 상태인지 알아야 하며 내게 친절하고 관대하게 대해야 한다고도 말했어. 대출을 받아야 할지도 모른다고 언질을 주었지. 그랬더니 거의 미친 듯이 화를 냈지 뭐야, 크리스티네. 나보고 생각이 없다면서 내 변덕스러움과 줏대 없음에 응하지 않는 것이 남편의 의무라고 말하는 거야. 나를 그렇게 봤던 거지. 그래서 생각했어, 남편을 구해야 한다고. 그렇게 어려움에서 벗어날 방법을 궁리하게 된 거야.

MRS LINDE.

And did your husband never get to know from your father that the money had not come from him?

NORA.

No, never. Papa died just at that time. I had meant to let him into the secret and beg him never to reveal it. But he was so ill then—alas, there never was any need to tell him.

MRS LINDE.

And since then have you never told your secret to your husband?

NORA.

Good Heavens, no! How could you think so? A man who has such strong opinions about these things! And besides, how painful and humiliating it would be for Torvald, with his manly independence, to know that he owed me anything! It would upset our mutual relations altogether; our beautiful happy home would no longer be what it is now.

MRS LINDE.

Do you mean never to tell him about it?

린데 부인

그럼, 남편은 그 돈이 네 아버지로부터 온 게 아니라는 것을 전혀 모르고 있니?

노라

응, 전혀. 아버지는 그 무렵에 바로 돌아가셨거든. 아버지께 사실을 알리고 절대 모르게 해달라고 부탁할 생각이었어. 그런데 병환이 너무 깊어져서 슬프게도 그렇게 말할 필요가 없어져 버렸어.

린데 부인

그럼 그때 이후로 남편에게 비밀을 말하지 않았니?

노라

세상에 어떻게 그런 생각을 하니? 그이는 이런 일에 아주 확고하거든. 게다가 남자로서 자존심 때문에 내게 빚진 것이 있다는 것을 알면 토르발이 얼마나 고통스럽고 치욕스러워하겠니! 우리의 관계는 끝장나고 아름답고 행복한 우리 가정도 더 이상 지금과 같지 않을 거야.

린데 부인

그 일을 남편에게 절대 말하지 않을 생각이야?

NORA.

[meditatively, and with a half smile]. Yes—someday, perhaps, after many years, when I am no longer as nice-looking as I am now. Don't laugh at me! I mean, of course, when Torvald is no longer as devoted to me as he is now; when my dancing and dressing-up and reciting have palled on him; then it may be a good thing to have something in reserve—[Breaking off.] What nonsense! That time will never come. Now, what do you think of my great secret, Christine? Do you still think I am of no use? I can tell you, too, that this affair has caused me a lot of worry. It has been by no means easy for me to meet my engagements punctually. I may tell you that there is something that is called, in business, quarterly interest, and another thing called payment in installments, and it is always so dreadfully difficult to manage them. I have had to save a little here and there, where I could, you understand. I have not been able to put aside much from my housekeeping money, for Torvald must have a good table. I couldn't let my children be shabbily dressed; I have felt obliged to use up all he gave me for them, the sweet little darlings!

노라

(생각에 잠기며 반쯤 미소를 짓는다) 글쎄, 아마도 언젠가 말하겠지. 수년이 지난 후 내가 지금처럼 더 이상 예쁘지 않을 때 말이야. 웃지 마! 그이가 지금처럼 나에게 빠지지 않을 때, 내가 춤추고 치장하고 연극을 해도 싫증이 날 때가 되면 그때 뭔가 얘깃거리로 좋을 것 같아. (갑자기 말을 멈춘다) 말도 안 돼! 그런 때는 절대 오지 않아. 자, 나의 큰 비밀을 어떻게 생각해, 크리스티네? 아직도 내가 쓸모없다고 생각하니? 사실, 난 정말 이 일 때문에 엄청나게 걱정하고 있단다. 기일을 꼬박꼬박 지킨다는 것은 정말 쉬운 일이 아니었어. 이자를 분기별로 납부하고 원금을 분할해서 내는 것도 있는데 매번 관리하기가 어찌나 어렵던지. 내가 할 수 있는 한 여기저기서 조금씩 아껴야만 했어. 생활비에서 따로 쓸 여유가 없었어, 토르발을 위해 좋은 음식을 차려야 했고 아이들도 초라하게 입힐 수 없었으니까. 그이가 우리 귀여운 아이들을 위해 준 돈은 꼭 써야 한다고 생각했어!

MRS LINDE.

So it has all had to come out of your own necessaries of life, poor Nora?

NORA.

Of course. Besides, I was the one responsible for it. Whenever Torvald has given me money for new dresses and such things, I have never spent more than half of it; I have always bought the simplest and cheapest things. Thank Heaven, any clothes look well on me, and so Torvald has never noticed it. But it was often very hard on me, Christine—because it is delightful to be really well dressed, isn't it?

MRS LINDE.

Quite so.

NORA.

Well, then I have found other ways of earning money. Last winter I was lucky enough to get a lot of copying to do; so I locked myself up and sat writing every evening until quite late at night. Many a time I was desperately tired; but all the same it was a tremendous pleasure to sit there working and earning money. It was like being a man.

린데 부인

그럼 그 돈은 모두 네 용돈에서 나온 거구나, 가엾은 노라?

노라

물론이지. 게다가 난 그 돈을 책임져야 할 사람이었으니까. 토르발이 새 옷이라도 사 입으라고 돈을 줄 때마다 나는 그 돈 절반 이상은 절대 쓰지 않았어. 가장 평범하고 저렴한 것들로 항상 구입했지. 다행스럽게도 어떤 옷이든 잘 어울렸고 토르발이 전혀 눈치채지 못했어. 하지만 크리스티네, 가끔 너무 힘들게 느껴졌어. 잘 차려입는 것은 즐거운 일이니까, 그렇지 않니?

린데 부인

그렇고말고.

노라

그리고 다른 부업도 찾았어. 지난겨울에 운이 좋게도 원고작업을 많이 받았지. 그래서 방안에 틀어박혀 저녁부터 늦은 밤까지 앉아서 날마다 글을 썼어. 몹시나 피곤함을 자주 느꼈지만 그래도 앉아서 돈을 번다는 건 굉장히 기쁜 일이었어. 마치 남자가 된 것처럼 말이야.

MRS LINDE.

How much have you been able to pay off in that way?

NORA.

I can't tell you exactly. You see, it is very difficult to keep an account of a business matter of that kind. I only know that I have paid every penny that I could scrape together. Many a time I was at my wits' end. [Smiles.] Then I used to sit here and imagine that a rich old gentleman had fallen in love with me—

MRS LINDE.

What! Who was it?

NORA.

Be quiet!—that he had died; and that when his will was opened it contained, written in big letters, the instruction: "The lovely Mrs Nora Helmer is to have all I possess paid over to her at once in cash."

MRS LINDE.

But, my dear Nora—who could the man be?

린데 부인

그렇게 해서 얼마나 갚았니?

노라

정확하게는 말할 수 없어. 그런 일을 기록하는 것은 정말 어려운 일이잖아. 내가 할 수 있는 한 모든 돈을 긁어모아 갚았다는 것만 알아. 어찌해야 할지 몰라 막막할 때가 많았어. (웃는다) 그때 여기에 앉아서 돈 많은 신사가 내게 반하는 상상을 하곤 했지…….

린데 부인

뭐라고! 누구야?

노라

쉿 조용! 그 신사가 죽고 난 후 유언장을 보니 큰 글씨로 "사랑하는 노라 헬머 부인에게 내 유산 전부를 즉시 현금으로 바칩니다"라고 쓰여 있는 거지.

린데 부인

어머, 세상에 노라! 그분은 누군데?

NORA.

Good gracious, can't you understand? There was no old gentleman at all; it was only something that I used to sit here and imagine, when I couldn't think of any way of procuring money. But it's all the same now; the tiresome old person can stay where he is, as far as I am concerned; I don't care about him or his will either, for I am free from care now. [Jumps up.] My goodness, it's delightful to think of, Christine! Free from care! To be able to be free from care, quite free from care; to be able to play and romp with the children; to be able to keep the house beautifully and have everything just as Torvald likes it! And, think of it, soon the spring will come and the big blue sky! Perhaps we shall be able to take a little trip—perhaps I shall see the sea again! Oh, it's a wonderful thing to be alive and be happy. [A bell is heard in the hall.]

MRS LINDE.

[rising]. There is the bell; perhaps I had better go.

NORA.

No, don't go; no one will come in here; it is sure to be for Torvald.

노라

맙소사! 못 알아듣겠니! 늙은 신사는 없어. 돈 구할 방법이 도저히 생각나지 않을 때 여기 앉아서 그런 생각을 해봤을 뿐이야. 하지만 이제 아무래도 좋아. 귀찮은 노인네가 어디에 있건 나는 늙은 신사나 그 유언장 모두 관심 없어. 이제부터 근심 걱정이 없기 때문이야. (벌떡 일어선다) 아, 생각하니 정말 기뻐, 크리스티네! 근심 걱정 없이 아이들과 뛰어놀 수 있어. 근심 걱정 없이! 근심 걱정 없이 집안을 예쁘게 가꾸고 토르발이 좋아하는 대로 모든 것을 가질 수 있어. 그리고 생각해 보니 곧 봄이 오고 넓고 푸른 하늘을 볼 수 있겠네! 아마도 우리는 짧은 여행을 떠날 수 있어, 바다를 다시 볼 수 있어! 아, 살아있고 행복하다는 것은 아주 멋진 일이야. (현관에서 벨이 울린다)

린데 부인

(일어서며) 벨이 울리네, 아무래도 나는 가는 게 좋겠어.

노라

아니야, 가지 마. 아무도 여기 안 올 거야. 토르발 때문에 온 게 틀림없어.

MAID.

[at the hall door]. Excuse me, ma'am—there is a gentleman to see the master, and as the doctor is with him—

NORA.

Who is it?

KROGSTAD.

[at the door]. It is I, Mrs Helmer. [Mrs LINDE starts, trembles, and turns to the window.]

NORA.

[takes a step towards him, and speaks in a strained, low voice]. You? What is it? What do you want to see my husband about?

KROGSTAD.

Bank business—in a way. I have a small post in the Bank, and I hear your husband is to be our chief now—

NORA.

Then it is—

하녀

(현관문에서) 실례합니다, 마님. 어떤 신사분이 나리를 뵙고자 오셨는데요, 의사 선생님이 나리와 함께 계셔서…….

노라

누구시지?

크로그스터

(문에서) **접니다, 헬머 부인.** (린데 부인은 깜짝 놀라고 떨며 창문 쪽으로 몸을 돌린다)

노라

(그에게 한 걸음 다가서며 긴장되고 낮은 목소리로 말한다) **당신이셨어요?** 무슨 일이죠? 남편에게 무슨 볼일이라도 있으신가요?

크로그스터

은행 일입니다. 은행에서 말단직에 있죠. 당신 남편분이 이제 은행장이 되었다는 소식을 들었소.

노라

그런데요?

KROGSTAD.

Nothing but dry business matters, Mrs Helmer; absolutely nothing else.

NORA.

Be so good as to go into the study, then. [She bows indifferently to him and shuts the door into the hall; then comes back and makes up the fire in the stove.]

MRS LINDE.

Nora—who was that man?

NORA.

A lawyer, of the name of Krogstad.

MRS LINDE.

Then it really was he.

NORA.

Do you know the man?

MRS LINDE.

I used to—many years ago. At one time he was a solicitor's clerk in our town.

크로그스터

그저 업무 때문에 왔습니다, 헬머 부인. 다른 용건은 없습니다.

노라

그럼 서재로 들어가세요. (노라는 냉담하게 인사하고 현관으로 가서 문을 닫는다. 다시 돌아와 난로에 불을 지핀다)

린데 부인

노라, 그 사람 누구였니?

노라

변호사인데 이름은 크로그스터야.

린데 부인

정말 그였구나.

노라

아는 사람이야?

린데 부인

몇 년 전에 알았어. 그때 우리 동네 법률 사무소 서기로 있었지.

NORA.

Yes, he was.

MRS LINDE.

He is greatly altered.

NORA.

He made a very unhappy marriage.

MRS LINDE.

He is a widower now, isn't he?

NORA.

With several children. There now, it is burning up. [Shuts the door of the stove and moves the rocking-chair aside.]

MRS LINDE.

They say he carries on various kinds of business.

NORA.

Really! Perhaps he does; I don't know anything about it. But don't let us think of business; it is so tiresome.

노라

그래, 그 사람이야.

린데 부인

아주 많이 변했네.

노라

불행한 결혼생활을 했거든.

린데 부인

그럼, 지금 혼자 된 거야?

노라

아이들이 있어. 이제 됐어, 타고 있군. (난로 문을 닫고 흔들의자를 한쪽으로 옮긴다)

린데 부인

사람들 말로는 그가 여러 가지 사업에 손을 댄다고 하던데.

노라

정말! 그럴지도 모르지. 그 일에 대해서 난 아무것도 몰라. 그런데 사업은 그만 생각하자, 재미없거든.

DOCTOR RANK.

[comes out of HELMER'S study. Before he shuts the door he calls to him]. No, my dear fellow, I won't disturb you; I would rather go in to your wife for a little while. [Shuts the door and sees Mrs LINDE.] I beg your pardon; I am afraid I am disturbing you too.

NORA.

No, not at all. [Introducing him]. Doctor Rank, Mrs Linde.

RANK.

I have often heard Mrs Linde's name mentioned here. I think I passed you on the stairs when I arrived, Mrs Linde?

MRS LINDE.

Yes, I go up very slowly; I can't manage stairs well.

RANK.

Ah! some slight internal weakness?

랑크 의사

(헬머 서재에서 나온다. 문을 닫기 전에 헬머에게 큰 소리로 말한다) 아니야 친구, 방해하지 않겠네. 잠시 부인한테 가 있겠네. (문을 닫고 린데 부인을 본다) 실례합니다, 여기도 손님이 계셨군요.

노라

아니요, 괜찮아요. (랑크를 소개한다) 랑크 의사 선생님이야. 이쪽은 린데 부인.

랑크

몇 번 린데 부인 성함을 들은 적이 있습니다. 제가 도착했을 때 계단에서 지나친 것 같은데요, 린데 부인?

린데 부인

네, 제가 너무 천천히 올라왔어요. 계단 딛기도 힘들어서요.

랑크

오, 저런! 어디 불편하신 데라도 있어요?

MRS LINDE.

No, the fact is I have been overworking myself.

RANK.

Nothing more than that? Then I suppose you have come to town to amuse yourself with our entertainments?

MRS LINDE.

I have come to look for work.

RANK.

Is that a good cure for overwork?

MRS LINDE.

One must live, Doctor Rank.

RANK.

Yes, the general opinion seems to be that it is necessary.

NORA.

Look here, Doctor Rank—you know you want to live.

린데 부인

아니요, 사실 제가 과로를 해서요.

랑크

더 편찮으신 데는 없어요? 그럼, 이곳에 휴양하러 오신 거군요?

린데 부인

일자리 알아보려고 왔어요.

랑크

일이 과로에 좋은 처방인가요?

린데 부인

살아야 하니까요, 랑크 선생님.

랑크

그렇죠, 대부분 사람이 그렇게 생각하죠.

노라

어머나, 선생님. 선생님도 살고 싶으시잖아요.

RANK.

Certainly. However wretched I may feel, I want to prolong the agony as long as possible. All my patients are like that. And so are those who are morally diseased; one of them, and a bad case too, is at this very moment with Helmer—

MRS LINDE.

[sadly]. Ah!

NORA.

Whom do you mean?

RANK.

A lawyer of the name of Krogstad, a fellow you don't know at all. He suffers from a diseased moral character, Mrs Helmer; but even he began talking of its being highly important that he should live. begin

NORA.

Did he? What did he want to speak to Torvald about?

랑크

물론이오. 아무리 비참하게 느낄지라도 가능한 한 오래 고통을 연장하고 싶소. 내 환자들도 모두 그렇소. 그리고 도덕적으로 병든 사람도 그렇죠. 안 좋은 상태에 있는 그들 중 한 명이 현재 헬머와 함께 있소.

린데 부인

(슬퍼하며) 아!

노라

누구 말씀하시는 거예요?

랑크

크로그스터라는 변호사 말이요. 부인께서 전혀 그 친구를 모르시는군요. 인격적으로 문제가 있는 놈이요, 헬머 부인. 그런 놈조차도 자신이 사는 것이 매우 중요하다고 지껄이기 시작했소.

노라

그가요? 그 사람이 토르발에게 무슨 말을 하고 싶어서 왔나요?

RANK.

I have no idea; I only heard that it was something about the Bank.

NORA.

I didn't know this—what's his name—Krogstad had anything to do with the Bank.

RANK.

Yes, he has some sort of appointment there. [To Mrs Linde.] I don't know whether you find also in your part of the world that there are certain people who go zealously snuffing about to smell out moral corruption, and, as soon as they have found some, put the person concerned into some lucrative position where they can keep their eye on him. Healthy natures are left out in the cold.

MRS LINDE.

Still I think the sick are those who most need taking care of.

랑크

잘 모르겠소, 단지 은행 일 때문에 온 것이라고 들었소.

노라

저는 몰랐는데요, 이름이 뭐더라 …… 크로그스터 씨가 은행과 관련이 있다는 것을 말이에요.

랑크

네, 그는 은행에서 직책을 맡고 있죠. (린데 부인에게) 부인께서 사시는 지역에도 있을지 모르겠습니다만 남의 도덕적 부패를 알아내려고 열심히 킁킁거리며 냄새를 맡고 다니는 사람들이죠. 그러다가 그런 사람을 찾아내면 자신들이 그를 감시할 수 있는 유리한 지위에 밀어 넣어 버린답니다. 선량한 사람들은 뒤로 물러날 수밖에 없고요.

린데 부인

그런 사람들이 가장 먼저 치료받아야 할 환자라고 생각해요.

RANK.

[shrugging his shoulders]. Yes, there you are. That is the sentiment that is turning Society into a sick-house.

[NORA, who has been absorbed in her thoughts, breaks out into smothered laughter and claps her hands.]

RANK.

Why do you laugh at that? Have you any notion what Society really is?

NORA.

What do I care about tiresome Society? I am laughing at something quite different, something extremely amusing. Tell me, Doctor Rank, are all the people who are employed in the Bank dependent on Torvald now?

RANK.

Is that what you find so extremely amusing?

NORA.

[smiling and humming]. That's my affair! [Walking about the room.] It's perfectly glorious to think that we have— that Torvald has so much power over so many people.

랑크

(어깨를 으쓱하며) 네, 그렇죠. 그런 사고 때문에 사회가 병들어 가고 있죠.

(노라는 생각에 잠겨 있다가 갑자기 웃으며 손벽을 친다)

랑크

왜 그렇게 웃는 거죠? 사회가 정말로 어떤 것인지 아시오?

노라

지루한 사회에 제가 무슨 관심이 있겠어요? 제가 웃는 것은 전혀 다른 일로, 매우 즐거운 일 때문이에요. 은행에 고용된 모든 사람은 이제 토르발에게 달려있나요?

랑크

그게 그렇게 즐거운 일인가요?

노라

(미소를 지으며 콧노래를 부른다) 제 일이니 모르셔도 돼요. (방안을 돌아다닌다) 우리들, 아니 토르발이 많은 사람에게 권력을 가지고 있다고 생각하니 정말 영광스러워요.

[Takes the packet from her pocket.] Doctor Rank, what do you say to a macaroon?

RANK.

What, macaroons? I thought they were forbidden here.

NORA.

Yes, but these are some Christine gave me.

MRS LINDE.

What! I?—

NORA.

Oh, well, don't be alarmed! You couldn't know that Torvald had forbidden them. I must tell you that he is afraid they will spoil my teeth. But, bah!—once in a way —That's so, isn't it, Doctor Rank? By your leave! [Puts a macaroon into his mouth.] You must have one too, Christine. And I shall have one, just a little one—or at most two. [Walking about.] I am tremendously happy. There is just one thing in the world now that I should dearly love to do.

(주머니에서 봉지를 꺼낸다) 선생님, 마카롱 좀 드시겠어요?

랑크

뭐, 마카롱이요? 마카롱은 이 집에서 안 될 텐데.

노라

맞아요, 하지만 이건 크리스티네가 제게 준 것이에요.

린데 부인

뭐라고! 내가?

노라

오, 놀라지 마! 토르발이 마카롱을 허락하지 않는다는 걸 너는 몰랐으니까. 그이는 마카롱 때문에 내 이가 상할까 봐 염려하고 있 거든. 하지만 한 번 정도는 괜찮지 않나요. 선생님? 허락해 주신다 면! (마카롱을 랑크의 입에 넣는다) 너도 하나 먹어, 크리스티네. 그리 고 저도 하나 먹겠어요, 아주 작은 걸로 하나 …… 아니 두 개까 지. (걷기 시작한다) 전 굉장히 행복해요. 이제 세상에서 가장 하고 싶은 것 딱 한 가지가 있어요.

RANK.

Well, what is that?

NORA.

It's something I should dearly love to say, if Torvald could hear me.

RANK.

Well, why can't you say it?

NORA.

No, I daren't; it's so shocking.

MRS LINDE.

Shocking?

RANK.

Well, I should not advise you to say it. Still, with us you might. What is it you would so much like to say if Torvald could hear you?

NORA.

I should just love to say—Well, I'm damned!

랑크

그게 뭐죠?

노라

하고 싶은 말이 있는데 토르발에게 제 말이 들리도록 말이에요.

랑크

그럼, 왜 말하지 않소?

노라

하지만 감히 말할 수 없어요. 정말 충격적이거든요.

린데 부인

충격적이라고?

랑크

그렇다면 말하지 않는 게 좋겠군요. 하지만 우리에게 말해도 괜찮아요. 토르발에게 들리도록 부인이 매우 하고 싶은 말이 무엇이죠?

노라

그냥 이렇게 말하고 싶어요. 이, 빌어먹을!

RANK.

Are you mad?

MRS LINDE.

Nora, dear—!

RANK.

Say it, here he is!

NORA.

[hiding the packet]. Hush! Hush! Hush! [HELMER comes out of his room, with his coat over his arm and his hat in his hand.]

NORA.

Well, Torvald dear, have you got rid of him?

HELMER.

Yes, he has just gone.

NORA.

Let me introduce you—this is Christine, who has come to town.

랑크

미쳤어요?

린데 부인

노라, 세상에!

랑크

말하세요, 그가 나타났어요!

노라

(마카롱을 감춘다) 쉬! 쉬! 쉬! (헬머가 팔에 외투를 걸치고 손에 모자를 들며 서재에서 나온다)

노라

어머, 토르발, 그를 돌려보냈나요?

헬머

응, 방금 떠났어.

노라

소개해 드릴 분이 있어요. 이분은 크리스티네, 조금 전에 도착했어요.

HELMER.

Christine—? Excuse me, but I don't know—

NORA.

Mrs Linde, dear; Christine Linde.

HELMER.

Of course. A school friend of my wife's, I presume?

MRS LINDE.

Yes, we have known each other since then.

NORA.

And just think, she has taken a long journey in order to see you.

HELMER.

What do you mean?

MRS LINDE.

No, really, I—

헬머

크리스티네? 실례합니다만 저는 잘 모르겠는데요…….

노라

린데 부인이에요, 크리스티네 린데.

헬머

아, 그렇군요. 집사람 학창 시절 친구분 맞으시죠?

린데 부인

네, 그때 이후로 서로 알고 지냅니다.

노라

그리고 잠깐, 당신에게 볼일이 있어 멀리서 오셨어요.

헬머

무슨 뜻이죠?

린데 부인

아니, 그게, 저…….

NORA.

Christine is tremendously clever at book-keeping, and she is frightfully anxious to work under some clever man, so as to perfect herself—

HELMER.

Very sensible, Mrs Linde.

NORA.

And when she heard you had been appointed manager of the Bank—the news was telegraphed, you know—she travelled here as quick as she could. Torvald, I am sure you will be able to do something for Christine, for my sake, won't you?

HELMER.

Well, it is not altogether impossible. I presume you are a widow, Mrs Linde?

MRS LINDE.

Yes.

HELMER.

And have had some experience of book-keeping?

노라

크리스티네는 서류 업무에 적임자예요. 그래서 업무를 더 익히고자 능력 있는 분 밑에서 일하고 싶어 해요.

헬머

참 좋은 생각이군요, 린데 부인.

노라

전보를 통해 당신이 은행장으로 임명되었다는 소식을 전해 듣고 서둘러 오신 거예요. 토르발, 크리스티네와 저를 위해서 뭔가 해줄 수 있다고 생각해요, 그렇죠?

헬머

글쎄, 안될 것도 없죠. 미망인이라고 알고 있는데요, 린데 부인?

린데 부인

네.

헬머

사무 업무 경험은 있으신가요?

MRS LINDE.

Yes, a fair amount.

HELMER.

Ah! well, it's very likely I may be able to find something for you—

NORA.

[clapping her hands]. What did I tell you? What did I tell you?

HELMER.

You have just come at a fortunate moment, Mrs Linde.

MRS LINDE.

How am I to thank you?

HELMER.

There is no need. [Puts on his coat.] But today you must excuse me—

RANK.

Wait a minute; I will come with you. [Brings his fur coat from the hall and warms it at the fire.]

린데 부인

네, 어느 정도 했어요.

헬머

오! 그렇다면, 부인에게 일자리를 마련해 드릴 수 있을 것 같군요.

노라

(손뼉을 치며) 거 봐! 내가 뭐랬니?

헬머

마침 좋은 시기에 오셨어요, 린데 부인.

린데 부인

어떻게 감사의 말씀을 드려야 할지…….

헬머

그럴 필요 없어요. (코트를 입는다) 그런데 오늘 저는 이만 실례하겠습니다.

랑크

잠시 기다리게, 나도 같이 나가세. (현관에서 털외투를 가지고 와 난로에 따뜻하게 쬔다)

NORA.

Don't be long away, Torvald dear.

HELMER.

About an hour, not more.

NORA.

Are you going too, Christine?

MRS LINDE.

[putting on her cloak]. Yes, I must go and look for a room.

HELMER.

Oh, well then, we can walk down the street together.

NORA.

[helping her]. What a pity it is we are so short of space here; I am afraid it is impossible for us—

MRS LINDE.

Please don't think of it! Goodbye, Nora dear, and many thanks.

노라

멀리 가지 마세요, 토르발.

헬머

한 시간 정도, 더 걸리지 않아.

노라

너도 가는 거니. 크리스티네?

린데 부인

(망토를 입으며) 응, 나가서 방 좀 구하려고.

헬머

그럼, 우리 모두 밖으로 나가는군요.

노라

(린데 부인을 거들며) 집이 좁아서 어쩔 수가 없네. 우리로서는 어떻게 해주지 못하고…….

린데 부인

그런 생각하지 마! 잘 있어. 노라, 여러 가지로 고마워.

NORA.

Goodbye for the present. Of course you will come back this evening. And you too, Dr. Rank. What do you say? If you are well enough? Oh, you must be! Wrap yourself up well. [They go to the door all talking together. Children's voices are heard on the staircase.]

NORA.

There they are! There they are! [She runs to open the door. The NURSE comes in with the children.] Come in! Come in! [Stoops and kisses them.] Oh, you sweet blessings! Look at them, Christine! Aren't they darlings?

RANK.

Don't let us stand here in the draught.

HELMER.

Come along, Mrs Linde; the place will only be bearable for a mother now!

[RANK, HELMER, and Mrs Linde go downstairs. The NURSE comes forward with the children; NORA shuts the hall door.]

노라

이따 또 만나. 물론 오늘 밤 돌아오겠지. 랑크 선생님도요. 뭐라
고요? 컨디션이 좋다면요? 틀림없이 좋으실 거예요. 몸을 따뜻하게
하세요. (모두 얘기를 나누며 현관으로 간다. 계단에서 아이들 목소리가 들
린다)

노라

왔구나! 왔어! (달려가 문을 연다. 유모가 아이들과 함께 들어온다) 들
어와! 어서! (몸을 굽혀 아이들에게 입을 맞춘다) 오, 예쁜 아이들! 애
들 좀 봐, 크리스티네! 사랑스럽지 않니?

랑크

찬바람 드는 곳에 서 있지 말아요.

헬머

어서 갑시다, 린데 부인. 여기는 아이들 엄마만 견딜 수 있는 곳
일 겁니다.

(랑크, 헬머, 린데 부인이 계단을 내려간다. 유모가 아이들을 데리고 간다.
노라는 현관문을 닫는다)

NORA.

How fresh and well you look! Such red cheeks like apples and roses. [The children all talk at once while she speaks to them.] Have you had great fun? That's splendid! What, you pulled both Emmy and Bob along on the sledge? —both at once?—that was good. You are a clever boy, Ivar. Let me take her for a little, Anne. My sweet little baby doll! [Takes the baby from the MAID and dances it up and down.] Yes, yes, mother will dance with Bob too. What! Have you been snowballing? I wish I had been there too! No, no, I will take their things off, Anne; please let me do it, it is such fun. Go in now, you look half frozen. There is some hot coffee for you on the stove.

[The NURSE goes into the room on the left. NORA takes off the children's things and throws them about, while they all talk to her at once.]

NORA.

Really! Did a big dog run after you? But it didn't bite you? No, dogs don't bite nice little dolly children. You mustn't look at the parcels, Ivar.

노라

너희들은 기운이 좋아 보이는구나! 볼이 사과와 장미처럼 빨갛네. (노라가 아이들에게 말하는 동안 서로 재잘거린다) 재미있었니? 정말 훌륭해! 네가 에이미와 보브를 썰매로 이끌었다고? 둘 다 한 번에? 잘했어. 너는 영리한 아이야, 이바르. 제가 막내를 안고 있을게요, 안네. 내 귀여운 아기! (유모에게서 아이를 받아 안고 흔들며 춤을 춘다) 그래, 그래 엄마가 보브하고도 춤을 출게. 뭐라고! 너희들 눈싸움 했다고? 나도 거기 있었으면 좋았을 텐데! 아니, 아니, 제가 벗길게요, 안네. 제가 하도록 놔두세요. 지금 들어가세요. 얼굴이 반쯤 얼었어요. 난로에 뜨거운 커피 있으니 마셔요.

(유모가 왼쪽 방으로 들어간다. 노라가 아이들을 벗기는 동안 아이들은 서로 재잘댄다)

노라

정말? 큰 개가 너희를 쫓아왔다고? 하지만 물지는 않았지? 그렇지, 개들은 귀엽고 작은 인형 같은 아이를 물지 않지. 포장된 것 보면 안 돼, 이바르.

What are they? Ah, I dare say you would like to know. No, no—it's something nasty! Come, let us have a game! What shall we play at? Hide and Seek? Yes, we'll play Hide and Seek. Bob shall hide first. Must I hide? Very well, I'll hide first.

[She and the children laugh and shout, and romp in and out of the room; at last NORA hides under the table, the children rush in and out for her, but do not see her; they hear her smothered laughter, run to the table, lift up the cloth and find her. Shouts of laughter. She crawls forward and pretends to frighten them. Fresh laughter. Meanwhile there has been a knock at the hall door, but none of them has noticed it. The door is half opened, and KROGSTAD appears, he waits a little; the game goes on.]

KROGSTAD.
Excuse me, Mrs Helmer.

NORA.
[with a stifled cry, turns round and gets up on to her knees]. Ah! what do you want?

무엇일까? 네가 알고 싶다는 것을 알아. 아냐, 약간 징그러운 것이야! 자, 우리 놀자! 뭐 하고 놀까? 숨바꼭질? 좋아, 우리 숨바꼭질하자. 바브부터 먼저 숨어. 엄마부터? 좋아, 엄마부터 숨는다.

(노라와 아이들은 웃고 소리 지르며 방을 들락날락하며 뛰논다. 마지막에 노라는 테이블 밑으로 숨고 아이들은 엄마를 찾으러 달려왔지만 보지 못한다. 아이들이 엄마의 킥킥 웃는 소리를 듣고 테이블로 달려가 테이블보를 들쳐 엄마를 찾는다. 웃음소리가 들린다. 노라는 아이들을 위협하듯이 엉금엉금 기어 나온다. 유쾌한 웃음소리. 현관에서 노크 소리가 나지만 아무도 알아채지 못한다. 문이 반쯤 열리고 크로그스터가 나타난다. 그는 잠시 기다리고 놀이는 계속된다)

크로그스터
실례합니다, 헬머 부인.

노라
(낮게 비명을 지르며 돌아보고 무릎을 꿇고 일어선다) **어머, 원하는 게 뭐죠?**

KROGSTAD.

Excuse me, the outer door was ajar; I suppose someone forgot to shut it.

NORA.

[rising]. My husband is out, Mr. Krogstad.

KROGSTAD.

I know that.

NORA.

What do you want here, then?

KROGSTAD.

A word with you.

NORA.

With me?—[To the children, gently.] Go in to nurse. What? No, the strange man won't do mother any harm. When he has gone we will have another game. [She takes the children into the room on the left, and shuts the door after them.] You want to speak to me?

KROGSTAD.

Yes, I do.

크로그스터

실례합니다, 바깥문이 열려 있어서 누가 문 닫는 것을 깜빡한 걸로 생각했어요.

노라

(일어나며) 남편은 외출했어요, 크로그스터 씨.

크로그스터

알고 있습니다.

노라.

그럼, 여기 무슨 용건이죠?

크로그스터

잠깐 말씀드릴 것이 있는데요.

노라

제게요? (아이들에게 나지막하게 말한다) 유모에게 가렴. 뭐라고? 아니야, 낯선 아저씨는 엄마에게 어떤 해도 끼치지 않는단다. 아저씨가 가시면 다른 놀이 하자. (노라는 아이들을 왼쪽 방으로 들여보내고 문을 닫는다) 저와 얘기하고 싶으시다고요?

크로그스터

네, 그렇습니다.

NORA.

Today? It is not the first of the month yet.

KROGSTAD.

No, it is Christmas Eve, and it will depend on yourself what sort of a Christmas you will spend.

NORA.

What do you mean? Today it is absolutely impossible for me—

KROGSTAD.

We won't talk about that until later on. This is something different. I presume you can give me a moment?

NORA.

Yes—yes, I can—although—

KROGSTAD.

Good. I was in Olsen's Restaurant and saw your husband going down the street—

노라

오늘요? 아직 초하루가 아닌데요.

크로그스터

그렇습니다, 오늘은 크리스마스이브지요. 어떤 크리스마스를 보낼지는 부인에게 달려있습니다.

노라

그게 무슨 말씀이죠? 오늘은 정말 안 돼요.

크로그스터

그 일에 관해서는 얘기하지 않을 겁니다. 이건 좀 다른 일입니다. 잠시 시간을 내주시겠어요?

노라

네, 그러죠. 다만 …….

크로그스터

좋습니다. 제가 올센 레스토랑에 있을 때 남편께서 외출하시는 것을 봤습니다.

NORA.

Yes?

KROGSTAD.

With a lady.

NORA.

What then?

KROGSTAD.

May I make so bold as to ask if it was a Mrs Linde?

NORA.

It was.

KROGSTAD.

Just arrived in town?

NORA.

Yes, today.

KROGSTAD.

She is a great friend of yours, isn't she?

노라

그런데요?

크로그스터

어떤 부인과 함께 말입니다.

노라

그래서요?

크로그스터

실례지만 그분 혹시 린데 부인 아닙니까?

노라

맞아요.

크로그스터

이 지역에 방금 도착하셨나요?

노라

네, 오늘이요.

크로그스터

부인 친구분 맞으시죠?

NORA.

She is. But I don't see—

KROGSTAD.

I knew her too, once upon a time.

NORA.

I am aware of that.

KROGSTAD.

Are you? So you know all about it; I thought as much. Then I can ask you, without beating about the bush—is Mrs Linde to have an appointment in the Bank?

NORA.

What right have you to question me, Mr. Krogstad?— You, one of my husband's subordinates! But since you ask, you shall know. Yes, Mrs Linde is to have an appointment. And it was I who pleaded her cause, Mr. Krogstad, let me tell you that.

KROGSTAD.

I was right in what I thought, then.

노라

네, 그런데 왜…….

크로그스터

저도 예전에 그분을 알았거든요.

노라

알고 있습니다.

크로그스터

그래요? 부인께서도 다 알고 계셨군요. 저도 그러리라 생각했어요. 그렇다면 단도직입적으로 묻겠습니다. 린데 부인이 은행에서 일하게 되는 건가요?

노라

무슨 권리로 제게 질문하시죠, 크로그스터 씨? 당신은 남편 부하 직원이잖아요. 하지만 물어보시니 알려드리죠. 맞아요, 린데 부인은 은행에서 일하게 될 거예요. 그리고 린데 부인 건으로 부탁한 사람은 저라는 것을 말씀드리죠, 크로그스터 씨.

크로그스터

제가 생각한 게 맞았군요.

NORA.

[walking up and down the stage]. Sometimes one has a tiny little bit of influence, I should hope. Because one is a woman, it does not necessarily follow that—. When anyone is in a subordinate position, Mr. Krogstad, they should really be careful to avoid offending anyone who— who—

KROGSTAD.

Who has influence?

NORA.

Exactly.

KROGSTAD.

[changing his tone]. Mrs Helmer, you will be so good as to use your influence on my behalf.

NORA.

What? What do you mean?

KROGSTAD.

You will be so kind as to see that I am allowed to keep my subordinate position in the Bank.

노라

(이리저리 돌아다니며) 때로는 누구나 작은 영향력을 가지기 마련이고 저 역시 그러길 바라요. 여자라는 이유로 반드시 따를 필요는 없어요. 크로그스터 씨, 남 밑에서 일하는 사람들은 다른 사람을 불쾌하게 하지 않도록 정말 조심해야 해요. 특히나 그 사람이······.

크로그스터

영향력 있는 사람 말인가요?

노라

그렇죠.

크로그스터

(말투를 바꾸며) 헬머 부인, 저를 대신해서 부인의 힘을 좀 써주실 수 있나요?

노라

네? 무슨 말씀이세요?

크로그스터

은행에서 제 자리를 유지하는데 부인께서 도와주실 수 있을 겁니다.

NORA.

What do you mean by that? Who proposes to take your post away from you?

KROGSTAD.

Oh, there is no necessity to keep up the pretence of ignorance. I can quite understand that your friend is not very anxious to expose herself to the chance of rubbing shoulders with me; and I quite understand, too, whom I have to thank for being turned off.

NORA.

But I assure you—

KROGSTAD.

Very likely; but, to come to the point, the time has come when I should advise you to use your influence to prevent that.

NORA.

But, Mr. Krogstad, I have no influence.

KROGSTAD.

Haven't you? I thought you said yourself just now—

노라

그게 무슨 의미죠? 누가 당신 자리를 빼앗으려 하나요?

크로그스터

계속 모른 척하실 필요 없어요. 부인의 친구분이 저와 어깨를 맞대며 일하게 되는 상황에 자신을 드러내고 싶어 하지 않는다는 것을 저는 잘 압니다. 그리고 누구 때문에 제가 해고당하는지도 잘 알고요.

노라

하지만 제가 장담하는데…….

크로그스터

그럴 수도 있지요. 하지만 요점은 그걸 막기 위해 부인의 힘을 써줍시사 하고 부탁할 시기가 왔다는 겁니다.

노라

그런데 크로그스터 씨, 저는 그럴 힘이 없어요.

크로그스터

힘이 없다고요? 방금 부인이 한 말은…….

NORA.

Naturally I did not mean you to put that construction on it. I! What should make you think I have any influence of that kind with my husband?

KROGSTAD.

Oh, I have known your husband from our student days. I don't suppose he is any more unassailable than other husbands.

NORA.

If you speak slightingly of my husband, I shall turn you out of the house.

KROGSTAD.

You are bold, Mrs Helmer.

NORA.

I am not afraid of you any longer. As soon as the New Year comes, I shall in a very short time be free of the whole thing.

노라

물론 당신이 제 말을 그렇게 해석하게 하려고 할 의도는 없었어요. 제가 남편에게 그런 영향력이 있다고 생각하시는 이유가 뭐죠?

크로그스터

오, 저는 학창 시절부터 부인의 남편을 알고 있죠. 다른 남자들보다 고집이 세다고는 생각하지 않습니다.

노라

남편에 대해 언짢게 말씀하시면 당신을 돌려보내겠어요.

크로그스터

용감하시군요, 헬머 부인.

노라

전 더 이상 당신이 두렵지 않아요. 새해가 되면, 곧 모든 것에서 자유로워질 테니까요.

KROGSTAD.

[controlling himself]. Listen to me, Mrs Helmer. If necessary, I am prepared to fight for my small post in the Bank as if I were fighting for my life.

NORA.

So it seems.

KROGSTAD.

It is not only for the sake of the money; indeed, that weighs least with me in the matter. There is another reason—well, I may as well tell you. My position is this. I daresay you know, like everybody else, that once, many years ago, I was guilty of an indiscretion.

NORA.

I think I have heard something of the kind.

KROGSTAD.

The matter never came into court; but every way seemed to be closed to me after that. So I took to the business that you know of. I had to do something; and, honestly, I don't think I've been one of the worst.

크로그스터

(자신을 가다듬으며) 잘 들어요, 헬머 부인. 만약 필요하다면 은행에서 저의 작은 자리를 위해서 인생을 걸고 싸울 준비가 되어 있소.

노라

그런 것 같아요.

크로그스터

단지 돈을 위한 것만은 아닙니다. 사실 돈은 저에게 중요한 일이 아닙니다. 다른 이유가 있죠. 음, 부인께 제 상황을 말씀드리는 것이 낫겠네요. 다른 사람들과 마찬가지로 부인도 아시다시피 오래전에 제가 경솔한 죄를 지었습니다.

노라

그런 말을 들은 것 같아요.

크로그스터

그 사건은 재판까지 가지 않았어요. 하지만 그 이후로 모든 일이 막혀버린 것 같아요. 그래서 부인이 아시는 일을 시작한 것입니다. 뭔가를 해야만 했고 솔직히, 제가 가장 나쁜 사람이라고 생각하지 않아요.

But now I must cut myself free from all that. My sons are growing up; for their sake I must try and win back as much respect as I can in the town. This post in the Bank was like the first step up for me—and now your husband is going to kick me downstairs again into the mud.

NORA.

But you must believe me, Mr. Krogstad; it is not in my power to help you at all.

KROGSTAD.

Then it is because you haven't the will; but I have means to compel you.

NORA.

You don't mean that you will tell my husband that I owe you money?

KROGSTAD.

Hm!—suppose I were to tell him?

하지만 이제 저는 그런 모든 일에서 발을 빼야 합니다. 자식들은 커가는데 아이들을 위해서라도 제가 할 수 있는 한 이 마을에서 명예를 회복하기 위해 노력해야 합니다. 은행의 직위는 제게 있어 그 첫걸음과 같은데 이제 부인 남편분이 저를 다시 걷어차 진흙탕으로 떨어뜨리려 합니다.

노라

하지만 저를 믿어주세요. 크로그스터 씨, 저는 당신을 도울 힘이 도저히 안 돼요.

크로그스터

그건 부인에게 의지가 없기 때문이죠, 그러나 저는 부인을 강제할 수단이 있습니다.

노라

제가 당신에게 대출받은 사실을 남편에게 말하려는 건 아니죠?

크로그스터

흠! 만약 말한다면요?

NORA.

It would be perfectly infamous of you. [Sobbing.] To think of his learning my secret, which has been my joy and pride, in such an ugly, clumsy way—that he should learn it from you! And it would put me in a horribly disagreeable position—

KROGSTAD.

Only disagreeable?

NORA.

[impetuously]. Well, do it, then!—and it will be the worse for you. My husband will see for himself what a blackguard you are, and you certainly won't keep your post then.

KROGSTAD.

I asked you if it was only a disagreeable scene at home that you were afraid of?

NORA.

If my husband does get to know of it, of course he will at once pay you what is still owing, and we shall have nothing more to do with you.

노라

당신에게 분명 수치스러운 일이 될 거예요. (흐느끼며) 나의 기쁨이자 자랑이었던 제 비밀이 추악하고 졸렬한 수단으로 남편이 알게 된다니, 그것도 당신에게서 말이죠! 저를 정말 궁지에 몰려고 하군요! 그러면 저는 끔찍할 정도로 난처한 입장에 처하고 말 거예요.

크로그스터

난처한 입장뿐일까요?

노라

(격렬하며) 그래, 해보세요! 그리고 그건 당신을 더 힘들게 할 거예요. 남편은 당신이 얼마나 불량한지 알게 되고 당신의 직위는 결코 지키지 못할 거예요.

크로그스터

부인이 두려워하는 일이 비단 가정불화만으로 그치는 일인지 질문드리는 겁니다.

노라

만약 남편이 알게 되면 즉시 잔금을 갚을 거예요. 그리고 우리는 더 이상 당신과 관계가 없을 거예요.

KROGSTAD.

[coming a step nearer]. Listen to me, Mrs Helmer. Either you have a very bad memory or you know very little of business. I shall be obliged to remind you of a few details.

NORA.

What do you mean?

KROGSTAD.

When your husband was ill, you came to me to borrow two hundred and fifty pounds.

NORA.

I didn't know anyone else to go to.

KROGSTAD.

I promised to get you that amount—

NORA.

Yes, and you did so.

크로그스터

(한 발짝 다가서며) 잘 들어요, 헬머 부인. 부인은 기억력이 나쁘거나 금전 거래에 대해 전혀 모르시는군요. 부인에게 좀 더 자세하게 설명해 드리죠.

노라

무슨 말씀이죠?

크로그스터

남편분이 병환으로 계실 때, 부인께서 250파운드를 빌리러 제게 오셨죠.

노라

누구에게 가야 할지 몰랐으니까요.

크로그스터

저는 그 금액을 드리기로 약속했고요.

노라

네, 그리고 이행하셨죠.

KROGSTAD.

I promised to get you that amount, on certain conditions. Your mind was so taken up with your husband's illness, and you were so anxious to get the money for your journey, that you seem to have paid no attention to the conditions of our bargain. Therefore it will not be amiss if I remind you of them. Now, I promised to get the money on the security of a bond which I drew up.

NORA.

Yes, and which I signed.

KROGSTAD.

Good. But below your signature there were a few lines constituting your father a surety for the money; those lines your father should have signed.

NORA.

Should? He did sign them.

KROGSTAD.

I had left the date blank; that is to say, your father should himself have inserted the date on which he signed the paper. Do you remember that?

크로그스터

저는 특정 조건으로 대출금을 드리기로 약속했습니다. 남편의 병환에 마음이 뺏기고 여비 마련에 노심초사해서 거래조건에는 주의를 집중하지 못하신 모양입니다. 그래서 제가 다시 한번 말씀드리는 것도 나쁘지 않을 것 같군요. 제가 작성한 채무증서를 담보로 돈을 마련하기로 약속했죠.

노라

네, 그래서 제가 서명했어요.

크로그스터

맞아요. 하지만 부인의 사인 밑에 몇 줄이 더 있는데 부인의 아버님이 보증인이 된다는 것과 아버님이 서명해야 할 사항이 있었습니다.

노라

그래서 아버님이 서명하셨지요.

크로그스터

저는 날짜를 빈칸으로 남겼습니다. 말하자면 부인의 아버님이 계약서에 사인하는 날짜를 직접 서명하시도록 한 겁니다. 기억나시죠?

NORA.

Yes, I think I remember—

KROGSTAD.

Then I gave you the bond to send by post to your father. Is that not so?

NORA.

Yes.

KROGSTAD.

And you naturally did so at once, because five or six days afterwards you brought me the bond with your father's signature. And then I gave you the money.

NORA.

Well, haven't I been paying it off regularly?

KROGSTAD.

Fairly so, yes. But—to come back to the matter in hand—that must have been a very trying time for you, Mrs Helmer?

노라

네, 기억합니다.

크로그스터

그런 다음, 부인 아버님께 우편으로 보낼 채무증서를 제가 부인께 드렸습니다. 그렇지 않나요?

노라

맞아요.

크로그스터

그리고 부인은 즉시 처리했는데 5, 6일 만에 아버님 서명이 있는 채무증서를 제게 가지고 오셨으니까요. 그러고 나서 제가 부인께 돈을 드렸죠.

노라

그런데, 제가 돈을 꼬박꼬박 갚고 있지 않나요?

크로그스터

그렇긴 하죠. 하지만 다시 본론으로 들어가서 부인께서는 힘든 시간을 겪고 계셨던 것 같습니다. 헬머 부인?

NORA.

It was, indeed.

KROGSTAD.

Your father was very ill, wasn't he?

NORA.

He was very near his end.

KROGSTAD.

And died soon afterwards?

NORA.

Yes.

KROGSTAD.

Tell me, Mrs Helmer, can you by any chance remember what day your father died?—on what day of the month, I mean.

NORA.

Papa died on the 29th of September.

노라

네, 그랬어요.

크로그스터

아버님도 매우 위독하셨고요, 그렇죠?

노라

거의 돌아가시기 직전이었죠.

크로그스터

그리고 곧 돌아가셨죠?

노라

네.

크로그스터

혹시 아버님이 돌아가신 날이 언제인지 기억할 수 있나요? 몇 월 며칠인지 말씀해 주세요.

노라

아버지는 9월 29일에 돌아가셨어요.

KROGSTAD.

That is correct; I have ascertained it for myself. And, as that is so, there is a discrepancy [taking a paper from his pocket] which I cannot account for.

NORA.

What discrepancy? I don't know—

KROGSTAD.

The discrepancy consists, Mrs Helmer, in the fact that your father signed this bond three days after his death.

NORA.

What do you mean? I don't understand—

KROGSTAD.

Your father died on the 29th of September. But, look here; your father has dated his signature the 2nd of October. It is a discrepancy, isn't it? [NORA is silent.] Can you explain it to me? [NORA is still silent.] It is a remarkable thing, too, that the words "2nd of October," as well as the year, are not written in your father's handwriting but in one that I think I know.

크로그스터

정확합니다. 저도 확인했거든요. 그런데 한 가지 이상한 점이 있는데(서류를 꺼내며) 도저히 이해가 안 됩니다.

노라

뭐가 이상해요? 저는 모르겠는데요…….

크로그스터

헬머 부인, 부인의 아버님이 돌아가신 지 사흘 후에 서명한 것으로 되어 있는 게 이상하지요.

노라

무슨 뜻이죠? 이해할 수 없어요.

크로그스터

부인의 아버님은 9월 29일 돌아가셨죠. 그런데 여기 보세요. 아버님께서 서명하신 날짜가 10월 2일로 되어 있어요. 이상하지 않나요? (노라는 말이 없다) 제게 설명 좀 해주시겠어요? (여전히 말이 없다) 연도뿐만 아니라 10월 2일이라는 글자도 눈에 띄게 부인 아버님 글씨체가 아니라 제가 알고 있는 글씨체입니다.

Well, of course it can be explained; your father may have forgotten to date his signature, and someone else may have dated it haphazard before they knew of his death. There is no harm in that. It all depends on the signature of the name; and that is genuine, I suppose, Mrs Helmer? It was your father himself who signed his name here?

NORA.

[after a short pause, throws her head up and looks defiantly at him]. No, it was not. It was I that wrote papa's name.

KROGSTAD.

Are you aware that is a dangerous confession?

NORA.

In what way? You shall have your money soon.

KROGSTAD.

Let me ask you a question; why did you not send the paper to your father?

뭐, 물론 이렇게 해석될 수 있어요. 부인의 아버님이 서명에 날짜 적는 것을 깜빡 잊으셨을 수도 있고 누군가 돌아가신 것을 알기 전에 아무렇게 작성했을 수도 있죠. 그게 나쁜 일은 아니죠. 문제는 아버님의 서명으로 그것이 친필인지에 달려있습니다. 여기에 서명된 이름, 아버님이 하신 건가요?

노라

(잠시 후. 고개를 들고 도전적으로 그를 보며) 아니요, 그렇지 않아요. 아버지 이름을 적은 것은 저예요.

크로그스터

위험한 자백이라는 것을 아시겠죠?

노라

어떤 점에서 그렇죠? 당신은 돈을 곧 가지게 되잖아요.

크로그스터

질문하나 하죠, 왜 아버님께 서류를 보내지 않으셨나요?

NORA.

It was impossible; papa was so ill. If I had asked him for his signature, I should have had to tell him what the money was to be used for; and when he was so ill himself I couldn't tell him that my husband's life was in danger—it was impossible.

KROGSTAD.

It would have been better for you if you had given up your trip abroad.

NORA.

No, that was impossible. That trip was to save my husband's life; I couldn't give that up.

KROGSTAD.

But did it never occur to you that you were committing a fraud on me?

NORA.

I couldn't take that into account; I didn't trouble myself about you at all. I couldn't bear you, because you put so many heartless difficulties in my way, although you knew what a dangerous condition my husband was in.

노라

어쩔 수 없었어요. 아버지 병세는 깊으셨는데 제가 만약 서명해 달라고 부탁한다면 아버지께 자금의 용도에 대해 말씀드려야 하잖아요. 아버지도 아프신데 남편 생명이 위독하다고 말할 수 없었어요. 정말 어쩔 수 없었어요.

크로그스터

차라리 해외여행을 포기하는 편이 나았을 텐데요.

노라

아니, 그렇게 할 수 없었어요. 여행하면 남편 생명을 구할 수 있는데 포기할 수 없었어요.

크로그스터

하지만 그런 일이 저를 속이는 행위라는 것을 전혀 생각해 본 적이 없나요?

노라

생각할 수가 없었죠. 당신에 대해 전혀 염려하지 않았어요. 남편이 위독한 상태인 줄 알면서도, 여러 가지 어려운 일들로 저를 매정하게 대했기 때문에 참을 수가 없었어요.

KROGSTAD.

Mrs Helmer, you evidently do not realise clearly what it is that you have been guilty of. But I can assure you that my one false step, which lost me all my reputation, was nothing more or nothing worse than what you have done.

NORA.

You? Do you ask me to believe that you were brave enough to run a risk to save your wife's life?

KROGSTAD.

The law cares nothing about motives.

NORA.

Then it must be a very foolish law.

KROGSTAD.

Foolish or not, it is the law by which you will be judged, if I produce this paper in court.

크로그스터

헬머 부인, 부인은 자신이 어떤 죄를 저질렀는지 명확히 깨닫지 못하는군요. 하지만 실수로 저의 명성을 완전히 잃어버린 것은 당신이 행한 일보다 그 이상도 그 이하도 아닌 똑같은 일이라는 것을 말씀드립니다.

노라

당신이? 당신 부인의 생명을 구하기 위해 위험에 달려들 정도로 용감했다는 것을 저에게 믿으라는 건가요?

크로그스터

법은 동기를 묻지 않아요.

노라

그렇다면 정말 엉터리 법률이군요.

크로그스터

엉터리 법률이거나 그렇지 않든 간에, 제가 이 서류를 법원에 제출하면 부인은 심판받게 됩니다.

NORA.

I don't believe it. Is a daughter not to be allowed to spare her dying father anxiety and care? Is a wife not to be allowed to save her husband's life? I don't know much about law; but I am certain that there must be laws permitting such things as that. Have you no knowledge of such laws—you who are a lawyer? You must be a very poor lawyer, Mr. Krogstad.

KROGSTAD.

Maybe. But matters of business—such business as you and I have had together—do you think I don't understand that? Very well. Do as you please. But let me tell you this—if I lose my position a second time, you shall lose yours with me. [He bows, and goes out through the hall.]

NORA.

[appears buried in thought for a short time, then tosses her head]. Nonsense! Trying to frighten me like that!—I am not so silly as he thinks. [Begins to busy herself putting the children's things in order.] And yet—? No, it's impossible! I did it for love's sake.

노라

믿을 수가 없군요. 딸이 죽어가는 아버지의 고통과 근심을 덜어드릴 수 없나요? 아내가 남편의 목숨을 구할 수 없나요? 법에 대해서 잘 모르지만 이와 같은 상황을 허용하는 법이 분명히 있다고 확신해요. 그런 법에 대한 지식도 없으면서 당신이 변호사인가요? 당신은 분명 무능한 변호사예요, 크로그스터 씨.

크로그스터

그럴지도 모르죠. 하지만 부인과 저 사이에 일어난 사건과 같은 문제들을 제가 이해하지 못한다고 생각하시나요? 좋습니다. 마음대로 하세요. 하지만 한 가지 말씀드리는데 만약 제 직위를 다시 잃게 된다면 저와 함께 부인의 자리도 잃게 될 것입니다. (묵례하고 현관을 지나 밖으로 나간다)

노라

(잠시 생각에 잠겨 있다가 머리를 치켜든다) 말도 안 돼! 그런 식으로 나를 협박하려는 거야! 그가 생각하는 것만큼 난 어리석지 않아. (아이들 물건을 치우며 분주해진다) 그렇다 하더라도? 아니야, 불가능해! 내가 사랑해서 한 일이야.

THE CHILDREN.

[in the doorway on the left]. Mother, the stranger man has gone out through the gate.

NORA.

Yes, dears, I know. But, don't tell anyone about the stranger man. Do you hear? Not even papa.

CHILDREN.

No, mother; but will you come and play again?

NORA.

No, no,—not now.

CHILDREN.

But, mother, you promised us.

NORA.

Yes, but I can't now. Run away in; I have such a lot to do. Run away in, my sweet little darlings. [She gets them into the room by degrees and shuts the door on them; then sits down on the sofa, takes up a piece of needlework and sews a few stitches, but soon stops.]

아이들

(왼쪽 출입구에서) 엄마, 모르는 아저씨가 문밖으로 나가셨어요.

노라

응, 알고 있어. 그런데 그 아저씨에 대해 아무에게도 말해서는 안 된다. 알았지? 아빠에게도 말이야.

아이들

네, 엄마. 다시 놀아줄 거예요?

노라

안 돼, 지금은 안 돼.

아이들

하지만, 엄마, 우리랑 약속했잖아요.

노라

그래, 하지만 지금은 안 돼. 안으로 가 있어. 엄마는 해야 할 일이 많아. 안으로 가 있으렴. 내 귀여운 아가들. (노라는 아이들을 방으로 서서히 들여보내고 문을 닫는다. 그런 다음 소파에 앉아 바느질을 시작하여 몇 땀을 놓다가 곧 멈춘다.)

No! [Throws down the work, gets up, goes to the hall door and calls out.] Helen! bring the Tree in. [Goes to the table on the left, opens a drawer, and stops again.] No, no! it is quite impossible!

MAID.

[coming in with the Tree]. Where shall I put it, ma'am?

NORA.

Here, in the middle of the floor.

MAID.

Shall I get you anything else?

NORA.

No, thank you. I have all I want. [Exit MAID.]

NORA.

[begins dressing the tree]. A candle here-and flowers here—The horrible man! It's all nonsense—there's nothing wrong. The tree shall be splendid! I will do everything I can think of to please you, Torvald!—I will sing for you, dance for you—[HELMER comes in with some papers under his arm.] Oh! are you back already?

안 돼! (일거리를 내던지고 일어나 현관문으로 가서 소리를 지른다) **헬**
렌! 크리스마스트리를 가지고 와. (왼쪽 테이블로 가서 서랍을 열고 다
시 멈춘다) **아니야, 아니야! 그건 정말 불가능해!**

하녀

(나무를 가지고 오며) **마님, 어디에 둘까요?**

노라

여기, 마루 한가운데.

하녀

뭐 또 다른 거 가지고 올까요?

노라

아니, 됐어. 필요한 건 다 있어. (하녀 퇴장)

노라

(나무를 장식하기 시작한다) **촛불은 여기에 놓고 꽃들은 이쪽에…….**
지독한 놈! 모두 엉터리야. 잘못된 건 없어. 크리스마스트리 정말
멋지겠다! 토르발, 당신을 기쁘게 하기 위해 무슨 일이든 할 거예
요. 당신을 위해 노래를 부르고 춤을 추겠어요. (헬머가 서류 뭉치를
팔로 안고 들어온다) **어머! 벌써 돌아오셨어요?**

HELMER.

Yes. Has anyone been here?

NORA.

Here? No.

HELMER.

That is strange. I saw Krogstad going out of the gate.

NORA.

Did you? Oh yes, I forgot, Krogstad was here for a moment.

HELMER.

Nora, I can see from your manner that he has been here begging you to say a good word for him.

NORA.

Yes.

HELMER.

And you were to appear to do it of your own accord; you were to conceal from me the fact of his having been here; didn't he beg that of you too?

헬머

응, 여기 누가 있었어?

노라

여기요? 아뇨.

헬머

이상하군, 크로그스터가 문밖으로 나가는 것을 봤는데.

노라

보셨어요? 아, 맞아요. 깜빡 잊었네요. 크로그스터 씨가 잠깐 들렀어요.

헬머

노라, 당신 태도를 보니 그가 당신에게 좋게 말해 달라고 부탁한 모양이야.

노라

그래요.

헬머

당신이 자진해서 한 것처럼 보이게 하라고, 자신이 여기에 왔다는 사실을 나에게 비밀로 하라고 당신에게 부탁하지 않았어?

NORA.

Yes, Torvald, but—

HELMER.

Nora, Nora, and you would be a party to that sort of thing? To have any talk with a man like that, and give him any sort of promise? And to tell me a lie into the bargain?

NORA.

A lie—?

HELMER.

Didn't you tell me no one had been here? [Shakes his finger at her.] My little songbird must never do that again. A songbird must have a clean beak to chirp with —no false notes! [Puts his arm round her waist.] That is so, isn't it? Yes, I am sure it is. [Lets her go.] We will say no more about it. [Sits down by the stove.] How warm and snug it is here! [Turns over his papers.]

NORA.

[after a short pause, during which she busies herself with the Christmas Tree.] Torvald!

노라

맞아요, 토르발, 하지만 …….

헬머

노라, 노라는 왜 그런 일에 관여하려고 하지? 그런 사람과 얘기하고 약속까지 해? 그리고 나에게 거짓말까지 하고?

노라

거짓말이라뇨?

헬머

여기에 아무도 없었다고 말하지 않았어? (노라에게 삿대질하며) 내 귀여운 작은 새는 그런 일을 다시 해서는 안 돼. 새는 깨끗한 부리로 재잘거려야지, 거짓말은 안 돼! (팔로 노라의 허리를 감싼다) 그렇지 않아? 그래, 나는 꼭 그렇다고 생각해. (노라를 놓아준다) 그런 얘기는 그만하지. (난로 옆에 앉는다) 여기는 정말 따뜻하고 포근해! (서류를 뒤적인다)

노라

(분주히 크리스마스트리를 장식하다가 잠시 멈추며) **토르발!**

HELMER.

Yes.

NORA.

I am looking forward tremendously to the fancy-dress ball at the Stenborgs' the day after tomorrow.

HELMER.

And I am tremendously curious to see what you are going to surprise me with.

NORA.

It was very silly of me to want to do that.

HELMER.

What do you mean?

NORA.

I can't hit upon anything that will do; everything I think of seems so silly and insignificant.

HELMER.

Does my little Nora acknowledge that at last?

헬머

응.

노라

내일모레 스텐볼크 씨 댁에서 가장무도회가 있는데, 전 정말 기대하고 있어요.

헬머

나도 당신이 무엇으로 나를 놀라게 할지 무척 궁금해.

노라

그런 것을 하고 싶어하는 제가 정말 바보 같았어요.

헬머

무슨 뜻이야?

노라

할 만한 것들이 떠오르지 않아요. 생각해 낸 것들이 모두 시시하고 하찮아요.

헬머

드디어 우리 노라가 그걸 깨달은 거야?

NORA.

[standing behind his chair with her arms on the back of it]. Are you very busy, Torvald?

HELMER.

Well—

NORA.

What are all those papers?

HELMER.

Bank business.

NORA.

Already?

HELMER.

I have got authority from the retiring manager to undertake the necessary changes in the staff and in the rearrangement of the work; and I must make use of the Christmas week for that, so as to have everything in order for the new year.

노라

(남편 의자 뒤로 서서 팔을 의자 등에 얹고) **많이 바쁘세요, 토르발?**

헬머

응.

노라

무슨 서류에요?

헬머

은행 업무야.

노라

벌써요?

헬머

퇴직하는 은행장으로부터 직원 인사이동과 업무 분장에 관해 필요시 변경하는 권한을 위임받았어. 크리스마스 휴일을 활용해서 새해까지 모두 정리해야겠어.

NORA.

Then that was why this poor Krogstad—

HELMER.

Hm!

NORA.

[leans against the back of his chair and strokes his hair]. If you hadn't been so busy I should have asked you a tremendously big favour, Torvald.

HELMER.

What is that? Tell me.

NORA.

There is no one has such good taste as you. And I do so want to look nice at the fancy-dress ball. Torvald, couldn't you take me in hand and decide what I shall go as, and what sort of a dress I shall wear?

HELMER.

Aha! so my obstinate little woman is obliged to get someone to come to her rescue?

노라

불쌍한 크로그스터 씨가 그랬던 이유가…….

헬머

흠!

노라

(남편 의자 뒤에 기대고 그의 머리를 쓰다듬는다) 만약 당신이 많이 바쁘지 않다면 매우 중요한 것 한가지 부탁드릴게요, 토르발.

헬머

뭐지? 말해 봐.

노라

당신처럼 좋은 감각이 있는 사람은 없어요. 이번 가장무도회에서 정말 멋지게 보이고 싶어요. 토르발, 제가 무엇으로 가장하고 어떤 옷을 입어야 할지 결정해 주시겠어요?

헬머

아하! 귀여운 고집쟁이 부인이 어쩔 수 없이 도움을 청하는 건가?

NORA.

Yes, Torvald, I can't get along a bit without your help.

HELMER.

Very well, I will think it over, we shall manage to hit upon something.

NORA.

That is nice of you. [Goes to the Christmas Tree. A short pause.] How pretty the red flowers look⸺. But, tell me, was it really something very bad that this Krogstad was guilty of?

HELMER.

He forged someone's name. Have you any idea what that means?

NORA.

Isn't it possible that he was driven to do it by necessity?

HELMER.

Yes; or, as in so many cases, by imprudence. I am not so heartless as to condemn a man altogether because of a single false step of that kind.

노라

네, 토르발. 당신 도움 없이는 조금도 어떻게 해야 할지 모르겠어요.

헬머

좋아, 한번 생각해 보지, 뭔가 떠오르는 게 있을 거야.

노라

당신은 좋은 분이세요. (크리스마스트리로 간다. 잠시 후) 빨간 꽃이 아주 예쁘네요. 그런데 크로그스터 씨가 저지른 일이 정말 나쁜 일이었나요?

헬머

그는 다른 사람의 이름을 위조했어. 그게 무슨 의미인지 알아?

노라

피치 못할 사정으로 그랬던 것이 아닐까요?

헬머

그럴 수도 있지만, 흔히 부주의로 발생하지. 나는 단 한 번의 잘못으로 어떤 사람을 정죄할 정도로 비정하지 않아.

NORA.

No, you wouldn't, would you, Torvald?

HELMER.

Many a man has been able to retrieve his character, if he has openly confessed his fault and taken his punishment.

NORA.

Punishment—?

HELMER.

But Krogstad did nothing of that sort; he got himself out of it by a cunning trick, and that is why he has gone under altogether.

NORA.

But do you think it would—?

HELMER.

Just think how a guilty man like that has to lie and play the hypocrite with every one, how he has to wear a mask in the presence of those near and dear to him, even before his own wife and children. And about the children—that is the most terrible part of it all, Nora.

노라

그래요, 토르발. 당신은 안 그러시겠죠, 그렇죠?

헬머

자기 잘못을 고백하고 처벌을 받아 평판을 회복하기도 한 사람들이 많이 있으니까.

노라

처벌이요?

헬머

그런데 크로그스터는 그렇게 하지 않았어. 교활하게 꼼수를 부려 빠져나가서 완전히 파산한 거야.

노라

하지만 정말 그런 거라고 생각하세요?

헬머

그런 죄를 지은 사람이 모든 사람에게 어떻게 거짓말을 하고 가식적으로 행동하는지 생각해 봐. 가까운 사람들, 자기 아내나 아이들 앞에서까지도 가면을 쓰면서 말이야. 아이들에게 가장 끔찍한 짓이지, 노라.

NORA.

How?

HELMER.

Because such an atmosphere of lies infects and poisons the whole life of a home. Each breath the children take in such a house is full of the germs of evil.

NORA.

[coming nearer him]. Are you sure of that?

HELMER.

My dear, I have often seen it in the course of my life as a lawyer. Almost everyone who has gone to the bad early in life has had a deceitful mother.

NORA.

Why do you only say—mother?

HELMER.

It seems most commonly to be the mother's influence, though naturally a bad father's would have the same result. Every lawyer is familiar with the fact.

노라

어째서요?

헬머

그런 거짓의 분위기가 집안 전체를 전염시키고 병들게 하니까. 그런 집안 아이들이 들이마시는 숨은 사악한 병균으로 가득 차 있지.

노라

(남편에게 가까이 다가서며) 그걸 확신하시는 건가요?

헬머

여보, 내가 변호사로 있을 때 수없이 봐왔어. 일찍이 타락한 사람들은 대부분 어머니가 거짓말쟁이야.

노라

왜 어머니로 단정하시죠?

헬머

일반적으로 어머니 영향을 많이 받으니까, 물론 나쁜 아버지도 같은 결과이긴 하지. 모든 변호사가 그런 사실을 알고 있어.

This Krogstad, now, has been persistently poisoning his own children with lies and dissimulation; that is why I say he has lost all moral character. [Holds out his hands to her.] That is why my sweet little Nora must promise me not to plead his cause. Give me your hand on it. Come, come, what is this? Give me your hand. There now, that's settled. I assure you it would be quite impossible for me to work with him; I literally feel physically ill when I am in the company of such people.

NORA.

[takes her hand out of his and goes to the opposite side of the Christmas Tree]. How hot it is in here; and I have such a lot to do.

HELMER.

[getting up and putting his papers in order]. Yes, and I must try and read through some of these before dinner; and I must think about your costume, too. And it is just possible I may have something ready in gold paper to hang up on the Tree. [Puts his hand on her head.] My precious little singing-bird! [He goes into his room and shuts the door after him.]

크로그스터는 거짓과 위선으로 끊임없이 자신의 아이들을 병들게 하고 있지. 그래서 그가 도덕성을 모두 잃었다고 말하는 거야. (자기 손을 노라에게 내민다) 그러니까 내 귀여운 노라는 그의 부탁을 들어주지 않겠다고 내게 약속해. 손을 내봐. 자, 자, 왜 그러지? 손을 내보라니까. 이제 됐어. 내가 그와 함께 일하는 것은 절대 불가능하다는 것을 확실히 말했어. 나는 그런 사람들과 함께 있으면 아주 기분 나빠.

노라

(남편에게서 손을 빼고 크리스마스트리 반대편으로 간다) **여기 정말 덥네요, 그리고 할 일도 많고요.**

헬머

(일어나서 서류를 정리한다) **좋아, 나도 저녁 식사 전까지 서류를 살펴봐야 하고 당신 의상도 생각해야지. 그리고 금종이 안에 넣을 것도 준비해서 트리에 매달아 놔야지.** (노라의 머리에 손을 얹는다) **내 소중한 종달새!** (그는 방에 들어가 문을 닫는다.)

NORA.

[after a pause, whispers]. No, no—it isn't true. It's impossible; it must be impossible.

[The NURSE opens the door on the left.]

NURSE.

The little ones are begging so hard to be allowed to come in to mamma.

NORA.

No, no, no! Don't let them come in to me! You stay with them, Anne.

NURSE.

Very well, ma'am. [Shuts the door.]

NORA.

[pale with terror]. Deprave my little children? Poison my home? [A short pause. Then she tosses her head.] It's not true. It can't possibly be true.

노라

(잠시 후. 속삭인다) 아니야, 아니야, 사실이 아니야. 그럴 리가 없
어! 절대 그럴 수가 없어!

(유모가 왼쪽 문을 연다)

유모

아이들이 엄마한테 가게 해달라고 조르는데요.

노라

아니, 안 돼요. 들여보내지 마세요. 애들과 함께 있어 주세요. 안
네.

유모

네, 마님 (문을 닫는다)

노라

(공포로 창백하다) 아이들을 타락시킨다고? 가정을 오염시킨다고?
(잠시 후. 노라는 머리를 든다) 사실이 아니야, 그럴 리가 없어!

ACT II

[THE SAME SCENE.—THE Christmas Tree is in the corner by the piano, stripped of its ornaments and with burnt-down candle-ends on its dishevelled branches. NORA'S cloak and hat are lying on the sofa. She is alone in the room, walking about uneasily. She stops by the sofa and takes up her cloak.]

NORA.

[drops her cloak]. Someone is coming now! [Goes to the door and listens.] No—it is no one. Of course, no one will come today, Christmas Day—nor tomorrow either. But, perhaps—[opens the door and looks out]. No, nothing in the letterbox; it is quite empty. [Comes forward.] What rubbish! of course he can't be in earnest about it. Such a thing couldn't happen; it is impossible— I have three little children.

[Enter the NURSE from the room on the left, carrying a big cardboard box.]

NURSE.

At last I have found the box with the fancy dress.

제2막

(같은 장면-피아노 옆에 크리스마스트리 장식이 벗겨졌고 헝클어진 가지에 촛불이 타다 남은 상태로 있다. 노라의 외투와 모자가 소파에 놓여 있다. 초조하게 방안을 홀로 걸어 다닌다. 소파 옆에 멈춰서 외투를 집어 든다)

노라

(외투를 놓는다) 누군가 지금 오고 있어! (문 쪽으로 가서 귀를 기울인다) 아니군, 아무도 없어. 당연하지, 오늘 크리스마스인데 누가 오겠어. 내일도 그렇고. 하지만 아마도 …… (문을 열고 밖을 내다본다) 아니야, 우편함에 아무것도 없어, 텅 비었어. (앞으로 나온다) 아무 소용도 없어! 당연히 그 사람이 진심으로 그럴 리가 없어. 그런 일은 일어날 수 없어, 불가능해. 나는 어린아이들이 셋이나 있다고.

(왼쪽 방에서 유모가 큰 종이상자를 들고 들어온다)

유모

가장무도회 의상이 있는 상자를 마침내 찾아냈어요.

NORA.

Thanks; put it on the table.

NURSE.

[doing so]. But it is very much in want of mending.

NORA.

I should like to tear it into a hundred thousand pieces.

NURSE.

What an idea! It can easily be put in order—just a little patience.

NORA.

Yes, I will go and get Mrs Linde to come and help me with it.

NURSE.

What, out again? In this horrible weather? You will catch cold, ma'am, and make yourself ill.

NORA.

Well, worse than that might happen. How are the children?

노라

고마워요, 테이블 위에 놓아주세요.

유모

(테이블 위에 놓는다) 그런데 수선 좀 해야겠어요.

노라

갈기갈기 찢어 버리고 싶군요.

유모

무슨 말씀을! 이건 쉽게 처리할 수 있어요. 조금만 참아요.

노라

아, 제가 린데 부인에게 가서 도와달라고 부탁해야겠어요.

유모

또 나가시게요? 이 추운 날씨에? 마님, 감기 걸리면 건강 해쳐요.

노라

글쎄요, 그것보다 나쁜 일이 일어날 수도 있어요. 아이들은 뭐하고 있어요?

NURSE.

The poor little souls are playing with their Christmas presents, but—

NORA.

Do they ask much for me?

NURSE.

You see, they are so accustomed to have their mamma with them.

NORA.

Yes, but, nurse, I shall not be able to be so much with them now as I was before.

NURSE.

Oh well, young children easily get accustomed to anything.

NORA.

Do you think so? Do you think they would forget their mother if she went away altogether?

유모

가여운 아이들은 크리스마스 선물 가지고 놀고 있어요, 그런데…….

노라

저를 찾나요?

유모

그렇죠. 아이들은 엄마하고 있는데 익숙해져서요.

노라

네, 하지만 유모, 이제부터 저는 예전처럼 아이들과 함께 오래 있을 수 없을 거예요.

유모

뭐, 어린아이들은 무엇이든 금방 적응하죠.

노라

그렇게 생각하세요? 엄마가 아주 멀리 가버리면 아이들은 엄마를 잊을까요?

NURSE.

Good heavens!—went away altogether?

NORA.

Nurse, I want you to tell me something I have often wondered about—how could you have the heart to put your own child out among strangers?

NURSE.

I was obliged to, if I wanted to be little Nora's nurse.

NORA.

Yes, but how could you be willing to do it?

NURSE.

What, when I was going to get such a good place by it? A poor girl who has got into trouble should be glad to. Besides, that wicked man didn't do a single thing for me.

NORA.

But I suppose your daughter has quite forgotten you.

유모

맙소사! 멀리 떠나다니요?

노라

유모, 제가 평소 궁금한 것이 있는데 대답해 줘요. 유모는 어떻게 자기 아이를 다른 사람에게 내맡길 수 있죠?

유모

어린 노라 아씨의 유모가 되려면 그렇게 할 수밖에 없었어요.

노라

그렇겠죠, 그런데 어떻게 그걸 기꺼이 할 수 있죠?

유모

뭐, 그때 이렇게 좋은 자리를 얻었잖아요? 어려운 처지에 있는 가난한 소녀는 이것도 감사해야죠. 게다가 그 나쁜 놈은 저를 위해 아무것도 하지 않았으니까요.

노라

그럼, 유모 딸은 유모를 아주 잊었겠군요.

NURSE.

No, indeed she hasn't. She wrote to me when she was confirmed, and when she was married.

NORA.

[putting her arms round her neck]. Dear old Anne, you were a good mother to me when I was little.

NURSE.

Little Nora, poor dear, had no other mother but me.

NORA.

And if my little ones had no other mother, I am sure you would—What nonsense I am talking! [Opens the box.] Go in to them. Now I must—. You will see tomorrow how charming I shall look.

NURSE.

I am sure there will be no one at the ball so charming as you, ma'am. [Goes into the room on the left.]

NORA.

[begins to unpack the box, but soon pushes it away from her].

유모

아뇨, 그렇지 않아요. 우리 딸은 세례를 받을 때나 결혼할 때 제게 편지를 보냈어요.

노라

(유모의 목을 껴안는다) 사랑하는 유모, 제가 어렸을 때 유모는 좋은 엄마였어요.

유모

가여운 노라 아씨에게는 저 말고 엄마가 안 계셨죠.

노라

만약 내 아이들이 엄마를 잃으면, 유모가 나를 대신해서……. 내가 도대체 무슨 쓸데없는 말을 하는 거야! (상자를 연다) 아이들에게 가줘요. 제가 얼마나 매력적인지 내일 보게 될 거예요.

유모

무도회에서 마님만큼 아름다운 사람은 아무도 없을 거라고 확신해요. (왼쪽 방으로 들어간다)

노라

(상자를 꺼내기 시작한다. 하지만 이내 내던진다)

If only I dared go out. If only no one would come. If only I could be sure nothing would happen here in the meantime. Stuff and nonsense! No one will come. Only I mustn't think about it. I will brush my muff. What lovely, lovely gloves! Out of my thoughts, out of my thoughts! One, two, three, four, five, six— [Screams.] Ah! there is someone coming—. [Makes a movement towards the door, but stands irresolute.]

[Enter Mrs Linde from the hall, where she has taken off her cloak and hat.]

NORA.
Oh, it's you, Christine. There is no one else out there, is there? How good of you to come!

MRS LINDE.
I heard you were up asking for me.

NORA.
Yes, I was passing by. As a matter of fact, it is something you could help me with. Let us sit down here on the sofa.

내가 과감히 나가버린다면. 아무도 오지 않는다면. 그 사이에 여기서 아무 일도 일어나지 않는다는 것을 확신할 수 있다면. 쓸데없는 소리! 아무도 오지 않을 거야. 생각해서는 안 돼. 목도리나 털어야지. 어머 예뻐라, 예쁜 장갑이야! 잊어버려, 잊어버리자! 1, 2, 3, 4, 5 (큰 소리를 낸다) 아, 누가 오는군. (문 쪽으로 움직이다가 망설이며 서 있다)

(린데 부인이 현관에서 외투와 모자를 벗고 들어온다)

노라

오, 너구나, 크리스티네. 밖에 또 누구 없지? 와줘서 고마워!

린데 부인

나를 찾았다고 들었어.

노라

응, 잠시 들렀어. 실은 네 도움이 필요한 일이 있어서. 소파에 앉자.

Look here. Tomorrow evening there is to be a fancy-dress ball at the Stenborgs', who live above us; and Torvald wants me to go as a Neapolitan fisher-girl, and dance the Tarantella that I learned at Capri.

MRS LINDE.
I see; you are going to keep up the character.

NORA.
Yes, Torvald wants me to. Look, here is the dress; Torvald had it made for me there, but now it is all so torn, and I haven't any idea—

MRS LINDE.
We will easily put that right. It is only some of the trimming come unsewn here and there. Needle and thread? Now then, that's all we want.

NORA.
It is nice of you.

MRS LINDE.
[sewing]. So you are going to be dressed up tomorrow Nora.

있잖아. 내일 저녁에 우리 위쪽에 살고 있는 스텐볼크 영사님 댁에서 가장무도회가 있는데 토르발은 내가 나폴리 어부 딸로 분장해서 카프리에서 배운 타란텔라 춤을 추길 원해.

린데 부인

알겠다, 네가 그 역할을 맡는구나.

노라

응, 토르발이 원해서. 봐봐, 이게 그 의상이야. 이탈리아에서 토르발이 내게 마련해준 거야. 그런데 지금은 너무 망가져서 어떻게 해야 할지 모르겠어.

린데 부인

쉽게 고칠 수 있어. 여기저기 실밥 나간 것만 손질하면 되니까. 바늘하고 실 있니? 그것만 있으면 돼.

노라

고마워.

린데 부인

(바느질하며) 그래서 내일 입을 예정이구나, 노라.

I will tell you what—I shall come in for a moment and see you in your fine feathers. But I have completely forgotten to thank you for a delightful evening yesterday.

NORA.

[gets up, and crosses the stage]. Well, I don't think yesterday was as pleasant as usual. You ought to have come to town a little earlier, Christine. Certainly Torvald does understand how to make a house dainty and attractive.

MRS LINDE.

And so do you, it seems to me; you are not your father's daughter for nothing. But tell me, is Doctor Rank always as depressed as he was yesterday?

NORA.

No; yesterday it was very noticeable. I must tell you that he suffers from a very dangerous disease. He has consumption of the spine, poor creature. His father was a horrible man who committed all sorts of excesses; and that is why his son was sickly from childhood, do you understand?

잠시 들러서 너의 멋진 모습을 봐야겠는걸. 그런데 어제 즐거운 저녁을 보낸 것에 고맙다는 말을 깜빡 잊었네.

노라

(일어서서 다른 쪽으로 간다) 글쎄, 어제는 다른 날보다 즐겁지 않았어. 네가 좀 더 빨리 왔어야 했는데, 크리스티네. 토르발은 집을 정말 기품 있고 멋지게 만들거든.

린데 부인

내가 보기에는 너도 그래. 네 아버님도 그러셨으니까. 그런데 랑크 선생님은 어제처럼 늘 우울하니?

노라

아니, 어제가 좀 심했어. 그분은 심한 질병을 앓고 있단다. 불쌍하게도 척추결핵이래. 그분의 아버지가 온갖 방탕한 짓을 저지르는 지독한 사람이었대, 그래서 아들이 어렸을 때부터 병약했던 이유야. 이해되니?

MRS LINDE.

[dropping her sewing]. But, my dearest Nora, how do you know anything about such things?

NORA.

[walking about]. Pooh! When you have three children, you get visits now and then from—from married women, who know something of medical matters, and they talk about one thing and another.

MRS LINDE.

[goes on sewing. A short silence]. Does Doctor Rank come here everyday?

NORA.

Everyday regularly. He is Torvald's most intimate friend, and a great friend of mine too. He is just like one of the family.

MRS LINDE.

But tell me this—is he perfectly sincere? I mean, isn't he the kind of man that is very anxious to make himself agreeable?

린데 부인

(바느질을 놓으며) 그런데 노라, 너는 어떻게 그런 것까지 알고 있니?

노라

(돌아다니며) 풋! 애가 셋이나 있으면 의료문제를 좀 아는 결혼한 여자들이 가끔 방문해서 이런저런 말을 한단다.

린데 부인

(바느질을 계속한다. 잠시 침묵이 흐른다) 랑크 선생님은 여기 매일 오시니?

노라

거의 매일 오셔. 그분은 토르발의 가장 친한 친구이고 나도 마찬가지야. 가족이나 다름없어.

린데 부인

그런데 그분은 정말 믿을만한 사람이야? 내 말은, 남의 비위를 잘 맞춰주는 그런 사람이 아니냐고?

NORA.

Not in the least. What makes you think that?

MRS LINDE.

When you introduced him to me yesterday, he declared he had often heard my name mentioned in this house; but afterwards I noticed that your husband hadn't the slightest idea who I was. So how could Doctor Rank—?

NORA.

That is quite right, Christine. Torvald is so absurdly fond of me that he wants me absolutely to himself, as he says. At first he used to seem almost jealous if I mentioned any of the dear folk at home, so naturally I gave up doing so. But I often talk about such things with Doctor Rank, because he likes hearing about them.

MRS LINDE.

Listen to me, Nora. You are still very like a child in many things, and I am older than you in many ways and have a little more experience. Let me tell you this—you ought to make an end of it with Doctor Rank.

노라

전혀 그렇지 않아. 왜 그렇게 생각하니?

린데 부인

어제 나를 소개할 때 그분은 내 이름을 이 집에서 몇 번 들었다고 말했어. 그런데 나중에 네 남편은 나에 대해서 아예 모르는 것 같았어. 그렇다면 랑크 선생님은 어떻게……?

노라

그건 맞아, 크리스티네. 토르발은 나를 정말 좋아해서 그의 말대로 나를 독차지하고 싶어 해. 처음엔 내가 고향에 있는 친한 사람 얘기만 꺼내도 거의 질투하는 것 같았어, 그래서 자연스럽게 나도 말하지 않게 되었지. 하지만 랑크 선생님과는 그런 얘기를 자주 해, 그분은 잘 들어주시니까.

린데 부인

잘 들어, 노라. 너는 여러 가지 면에서 아직도 어린아이 같아, 그리고 난 너보다 나이가 많고 경험이 좀 더 많아. 그래서 말하지만 랑크 선생님과의 일을 끝내야 해.

NORA.

What ought I to make an end of?

MRS LINDE.

Of two things, I think. Yesterday you talked some nonsense about a rich admirer who was to leave you money—

NORA.

An admirer who doesn't exist, unfortunately! But what then?

MRS LINDE.

Is Doctor Rank a man of means?

NORA.

Yes, he is.

MRS LINDE.

And has no one to provide for?

NORA.

No, no one; but—

노라

무엇을 끝내라는 거지?

린데 부인

내 생각에는 두 가지야. 돈 많은 사람이 너에게 많은 유산을 남기겠다고 어제 네가 이상한 말을 했잖아.

노라

그런 사람은 없어, 불행하게도! 그런데 그게 어떻다는 거야?

린데 부인

랑크 선생님은 돈이 많지?

노라

응, 그래.

린데 부인

그리고 부양할 사람도 없고?

노라

맞아, 아무도 없어, 그런데…….

MRS LINDE.

And comes here everyday?

NORA.

Yes, I told you so.

MRS LINDE.

But how can this well-bred man be so tactless?

NORA.

I don't understand you at all.

MRS LINDE.

Don't prevaricate, Nora. Do you suppose I don't guess who lent you the two hundred and fifty pounds?

NORA.

Are you out of your senses? How can you think of such a thing! A friend of ours, who comes here everyday! Do you realise what a horribly painful position that would be?

MRS LINDE.

Then it really isn't he?

린데 부인

그리고 여기 매일 오지?

노라

응, 그렇다고 말했잖아.

린데 부인

그런데 교양있는 분이 어떻게 분별없이 그럴 수가 있지?

노라

무슨 말인지 전혀 모르겠네.

린데 부인

얼버무려 넘기지 마, 노라. 누가 너에게 250파운드를 빌려줬는지 내가 모를 줄 아니?

노라

너 제정신이니? 어떻게 그런 생각을 하지? 그분은 우리 친구로 매일 여기에 오시는데! 그렇게 되면 얼마나 끔찍하게 곤란한 입장이 되겠니?

린데 부인

그러면 정말 그 사람이 아니니?

NORA.

No, certainly not. It would never have entered into my head for a moment. Besides, he had no money to lend then; he came into his money afterwards.

MRS LINDE.

Well, I think that was lucky for you, my dear Nora.

NORA.

No, it would never have come into my head to ask Doctor Rank. Although I am quite sure that if I had asked him—

MRS LINDE.

But of course you won't.

NORA.

Of course not. I have no reason to think it could possibly be necessary. But I am quite sure that if I told Doctor Rank—

MRS LINDE.

Behind your husband's back?

노라

아니고말고. 그건 생각지도 못한 일이야. 게다가 그때는 그분도 여유가 없었어. 유산도 나중에 받았는걸.

린데 부인

그럼, 다행이야, 노라.

노라

랑크 선생님께 부탁한다는 건 생각조차도 못 했지. 만약 부탁했더라면 틀림없이…….

린데 부인

하지만 그렇게 하지 않았지.

노라

물론이지. 그럴 필요가 있다고 생각할 수도 없어. 하지만 만약 그분께 말했다면 분명…….

린데 부인

남편에게는 비밀로 하고?

NORA.

I must make an end of it with the other one, and that will be behind his back too. I must make an end of it with him.

MRS LINDE.

Yes, that is what I told you yesterday, but—

NORA.

[walking up and down]. A man can put a thing like that straight much easier than a woman—

MRS LINDE.

One's husband, yes.

NORA.

Nonsense! [Standing still.] When you pay off a debt you get your bond back, don't you?

MRS LINDE.

Yes, as a matter of course.

노라

다른 사람과 그 일을 끝내야 해, 그것도 남편에게는 비밀이야. 그와 관계를 끝내야 해.

린데 부인

그래. 그건 내가 어제 말했잖아, 그런데…….

노라

(왔다 갔다 하며) 이런 일은 남자가 여자보다 잘 처리하겠지…….

린데 부인

남편이라면, 그렇겠지.

노라

말도 안 돼! (잠시 멈춘다) 빚을 갚으면 차용증서는 되돌려 받지 않니?

린데 부인

그래, 당연하지.

NORA.

And can tear it into a hundred thousand pieces, and burn it up—the nasty dirty paper!

MRS LINDE.

[looks hard at her, lays down her sewing and gets up slowly]. Nora, you are concealing something from me.

NORA.

Do I look as if I were?

MRS LINDE.

Something has happened to you since yesterday morning. Nora, what is it?

NORA.

[going nearer to her]. Christine! [Listens.] Hush! there's Torvald come home. Do you mind going in to the children for the present? Torvald can't bear to see dressmaking going on. Let Anne help you.

노라

그러면 차용증서를 갈기갈기 찢어서 태워 버릴 수도 있겠군. 불쾌하고 더러운 종이 따위는 말이야!

린데 부인

(노라를 지그시 바라보고 바느질을 내려놓으며 천천히 일어선다) **노라, 너 뭔가 감추고 있구나.**

노라

그래 보이니?

린데 부인

어제 아침부터 무슨 일이 있었던 거야. 노라, 무슨 일이야?

노라

(린데 부인에게 다가가며) **크리스티네!** (귀를 기울인다) **쉿! 토르말이 집에 왔어. 잠시만 애들한테 가주겠니? 토르발은 바느질하는 거 보면 질색하거든. 안네가 도와줄 거야.**

MRS LINDE.

[gathering some of the things together]. Certainly—but I am not going away from here until we have had it out with one another. [She goes into the room on the left, as HELMER comes in from the hall.]

NORA.

[going up to HELMER]. I have wanted you so much, Torvald dear.

HELMER.

Was that the dressmaker?

NORA.

No, it was Christine; she is helping me to put my dress in order. You will see I shall look quite smart.

HELMER.

Wasn't that a happy thought of mine, now?

NORA.

Splendid! But don't you think it is nice of me, too, to do as you wish?

린데 부인

(흩어진 물건을 모으며) 그래. 하지만 우리가 서로 이야기를 매듭짓기 전에는 돌아가지 않겠어. (왼쪽 방으로 들어가자 헬머가 현관에서 들어온다)

노라

(헬머에게 다가가며) 무척이나 보고 싶었어요, 토르발.

헬머

옷 수선하는 사람이었어?

노라

아뇨, 크리스티네예요. 드레스 손질하는데 도와주고 있어요. 맵시 있는 저의 모습을 보게 될 거예요.

헬머

내 생각이 적절했지, 어때?

노라

꾕장해요! 당신이 바라는 대로 하니 저도 착하지 않나요?

HELMER.

Nice?—because you do as your husband wishes? Well, well, you little rogue, I am sure you did not mean it in that way. But I am not going to disturb you; you will want to be trying on your dress, I expect.

NORA.

I suppose you are going to work.

HELMER.

Yes. [Shows her a bundle of papers.] Look at that. I have just been into the bank. [Turns to go into his room.]

NORA.

Torvald.

HELMER.

Yes.

NORA.

If your little squirrel were to ask you for something very, very prettily—?

헬머

착하다고? 남편이 바라는 대로 해서? 글쎄, 요 귀여운 장난꾸러기, 당신이 그런 뜻으로 한 말이 아니라는 걸 알지. 암튼 방해하지 않겠어, 당신은 드레스를 입어 보고 싶어 할 테니까.

노라

일하시려고요?

헬머

응. (서류 꾸러미를 노라에게 보인다) 이것 좀 봐. 방금 은행에 갔다 왔어. (서재로 들어가려고 돌아선다)

노라

토르발.

헬머

응.

노라

만약 당신의 작은 다람쥐가 뭔가 부탁을 한다면?

HELMER.

What then?

NORA.

Would you do it?

HELMER.

I should like to hear what it is, first.

NORA.

Your squirrel would run about and do all her tricks if you would be nice, and do what she wants.

HELMER.

Speak plainly.

NORA.

Your skylark would chirp about in every room, with her song rising and falling—

HELMER.

Well, my skylark does that anyhow.

헬머

그게 뭔데?

노라

들어 주실 거죠?

헬머

우선, 그게 뭔지 들어봐야겠지.

노라

만약 당신이 다정하게 원하는 것을 들어주신다면 다람쥐는 구르고 온갖 재주를 보일 거예요.

헬머

솔직하게 말해 봐.

노라

당신의 종달새는 온 집안에서 높고 낮은 소리로 노래 부를 거예요.

헬머

뭐, 내 종달새는 늘 그렇게 하지.

NORA.

I would play the fairy and dance for you in the moonlight, Torvald.

HELMER.

Nora—you surely don't mean that request you made to me this morning?

NORA.

[going near him]. Yes, Torvald, I beg you so earnestly—

HELMER.

Have you really the courage to open up that question again?

NORA.

Yes, dear, you must do as I ask; you must let Krogstad keep his post in the bank.

HELMER.

My dear Nora, it is his post that I have arranged Mrs Linde shall have.

노라

저는 당신을 위해 요정 연기를 하고 달빛 아래서 춤을 추겠어요.
토르발.

헬머

노라, 오늘 아침, 내게 요청한 일을 말하려는 거 아니야?

노라

(그에게 가까이 다가가며) 맞아요, 토르발. 정말 간곡히 부탁드려
요…….

헬머

당신 정말 그 얘기 또 끄집어낼 배짱이야?

노라

네, 여보, 제 부탁 들어주셔요. 크로그스터를 은행에 그대로 있게
해주세요.

헬머

여보 노라, 린데 부인을 그 자리에 앉히는 거야.

NORA.

Yes, you have been awfully kind about that; but you could just as well dismiss some other clerk instead of Krogstad.

HELMER.

This is simply incredible obstinacy! Because you chose to give him a thoughtless promise that you would speak for him, I am expected to—

NORA.

That isn't the reason, Torvald. It is for your own sake. This fellow writes in the most scurrilous newspapers; you have told me so yourself. He can do you an unspeakable amount of harm. I am frightened to death of him—

HELMER.

Ah, I understand; it is recollections of the past that scare you.

NORA.

What do you mean?

노라

네, 그건 정말 고마워요. 하지만 크로그스터 대신 다른 직원을 해고하면 되잖아요.

헬머

이건 말도 안 되는 억지야! 당신이 그를 대신해서 말해주겠다는 분별없는 약속을 했기 때문에 내가…….

노라

그 이유가 아니에요, 토르발. 이건 당신을 위해서예요. 그 사람은 삼류 신문에 글을 쓰고 있다고 당신이 제게 말씀하셨죠. 그는 이루 말할 수 없을 정도로 당신을 해칠 수 있어요. 그가 무서워 죽겠어요…….

헬머

아, 알겠어. 당신을 위협하는 건 옛날 일에 대한 기억 때문이지.

노라

무슨 뜻이에요?

HELMER.

Naturally you are thinking of your father.

NORA.

Yes—yes, of course. Just recall to your mind what these malicious creatures wrote in the papers about papa, and how horribly they slandered him. I believe they would have procured his dismissal if the Department had not sent you over to inquire into it, and if you had not been so kindly disposed and helpful to him.

HELMER.

My little Nora, there is an important difference between your father and me. Your father's reputation as a public official was not above suspicion. Mine is, and I hope it will continue to be so, as long as I hold my office.

NORA.

You never can tell what mischief these men may contrive. We ought to be so well off, so snug and happy here in our peaceful home, and have no cares—you and I and the children, Torvald! That is why I beg you so earnestly—

헬머

물론 당신 아버님 일로 그렇지.

노라

네, 그래요. 악한 사람들이 아버지에 대해 썼던 기사, 그리고 얼마나 끔찍하게 비방했는지를 생각해 보세요. 만약 정부에서 당신을 보내 조사하지 않았다면, 그리고 당신이 아버지를 친절하게 도와주지 않았다면 그들은 아버지를 해고했을 거라고 생각해요.

헬머

사랑하는 노라, 아버님과 나 사이에는 중요한 차이가 있어. 아버님은 공무원으로서 혐의가 없다고 할 수 없어. 나는 달라, 그리고 재직하는 동안 자리를 쭉 유지하고 싶어.

노라

당신은 이 사람들이 무슨 일을 꾸며낼지 절대 알 수 없어요. 우리는 여기 평화로운 가정에서 넉넉하고 안락하고 행복하게 살아야 하잖아요. 당신과 나 그리고 아이들 모두 걱정 없이 말이죠. 토르발! 그래서 제가 간절하게 부탁드리는 거예요.

HELMER.

And it is just by interceding for him that you make it impossible for me to keep him. It is already known at the Bank that I mean to dismiss Krogstad. Is it to get about now that the new manager has changed his mind at his wife's bidding—

NORA.

And what if it did?

HELMER.

Of course!—if only this obstinate little person can get her way! Do you suppose I am going to make myself ridiculous before my whole staff, to let people think that I am a man to be swayed by all sorts of outside influence? I should very soon feel the consequences of it, I can tell you! And besides, there is one thing that makes it quite impossible for me to have Krogstad in the Bank as long as I am manager.

NORA.

Whatever is that?

헬머

당신이 그를 위해 호소하니까 내가 더욱더 그놈을 그냥 놔둘 수가 없어. 은행에서는 내가 크로그스터를 해고한다는 것이 이미 다 알려졌어. 새 은행장이 마누라 명령에 따라 생각을 바꿨다고 소문이라도 난다면…….

노라

그렇다면요?

헬머

물론, 고집쟁이 당신은 바라던 것을 얻겠지! 내가 모든 직원 앞에서 웃음거리가 된다고 생각해 봐, 사람들은 내가 온갖 외부 영향에 흔들리는 사람이라고 생각하겠지? 나는 그 결과를 곧 느끼게 되고 말이야, 게다가 내가 관리자로 있는 한 은행에 크로그스터를 도저히 놔둘 수 없는 이유가 한 가지 있지.

노라

그게 뭐죠?

HELMER.

His moral failings I might perhaps have overlooked, if necessary—

NORA.

Yes, you could—couldn't you?

HELMER.

And I hear he is a good worker, too. But I knew him when we were boys. It was one of those rash friendships that so often prove an incubus in afterlife. I may as well tell you plainly, we were once on very intimate terms with one another. But this tactless fellow lays no restraint on himself when other people are present. On the contrary, he thinks it gives him the right to adopt a familiar tone with me, and every minute it is "I say, Helmer, old fellow!" and that sort of thing. I assure you it is extremely painful for me. He would make my position in the Bank intolerable.

NORA.

Torvald, I don't believe you mean that.

헬머

그의 도덕적 결함은 부득이한 경우, 한 번쯤 눈감아 줄 수 있지만 말이야.

노라

그래요, 당신은 그럴 수 있지 않나요?

헬머

그리고 그가 일을 잘한다는 말도 들었어. 하지만 내가 학창 시절에 그를 알았지. 분별없는 교우 관계가 나중에는 종종 부담스러워지는 일이 되어버리지. 당신에게 분명히 말하는 게 낫겠어. 우리는 서로 매우 친밀했던 사이였지. 그런데 이 분별없는 놈이 다른 사람들이 있을 때도 조심성이 없어. 도리어 내게 친밀한 말투를 써도 되는 권리가 있다고 생각하나 봐. 매번 "어이, 헬머, 여보게"라고 말한단 말이야. 그건 내게 너무나 곤란한 일이야. 은행에서의 내 지위도 유지할 수 없게 만들지.

노라

토르발, 당신이 그렇게 말하니 믿기지 않는군요.

HELMER.

Don't you? Why not?

NORA.

Because it is such a narrow-minded way of looking at things.

HELMER.

What are you saying? Narrow-minded? Do you think I am narrow-minded?

NORA.

No, just the opposite, dear—and it is exactly for that reason.

HELMER.

It's the same thing. You say my point of view is narrow-minded, so I must be so too. Narrow-minded! Very well—I must put an end to this. [Goes to the hall door and calls.] Helen!

NORA.

What are you going to do?

헬머

믿어지지 않아? 왜 그렇지?

노라

그건 옹졸한 마음으로 보기 때문이죠.

헬머

무슨 말을 하는 거야? 옹졸한 마음? 내가 옹졸하다고 생각하나?

노라

아니, 그 반대에요. 여보…… 그리고 바로 그런 이유 때문이에요.

헬머

마찬가지야. 내 생각이 옹졸하다고 말했으니 그러면 나도 옹졸한 인간인 거지. 옹졸하다! 그래 좋아, 이 일을 끝내야겠어. (현관문으로 가서 외친다) 헬렌!

노라

뭐 하시게요?

HELMER.

[looking among his papers]. Settle it. [Enter MAID.] Look here; take this letter and go downstairs with it at once. Find a messenger and tell him to deliver it, and be quick. The address is on it, and here is the money.

MAID.

Very well, sir. [Exit with the letter.]

HELMER.

[putting his papers together]. Now then, little Miss Obstinate.

NORA.

[breathlessly]. Torvald—what was that letter?

HELMER.

Krogstad's dismissal.

NORA.

Call her back, Torvald! There is still time. Oh Torvald, call her back! Do it for my sake—for your own sake—for the children's sake! Do you hear me, Torvald?

헬머

(서류를 보며) 결정을 내리도록 하지. (하녀 입장) 이것 봐, 이 편지를 가지고 즉시 내려가. 배달원이 보이면 전해주고 빨리 보내달라고 말해줘. 주소는 거기 있어. 그리고 여기 돈.

하녀

네, 알겠습니다. (편지를 가지고 나간다)

헬머

(서류를 놓으며) 자, 됐지, 고집쟁이 마님!

노라

(숨죽이고 있다가) 토르발, 그게 무슨 편지였죠?

헬머

크로그스터 해고 통지서.

노라

다시 불러요, 토르발! 아직 시간이 있어요. 오, 토르발 다시 오라고 하세요! 저를 위해서! 당신을 위해서! 아이들을 위해서! 제 말 듣고 있나요, 토르발?

Call her back! You don't know what that letter can bring upon us.

HELMER.

It's too late.

NORA.

Yes, it's too late.

HELMER.

My dear Nora, I can forgive the anxiety you are in, although really it is an insult to me. It is, indeed. Isn't it an insult to think that I should be afraid of a starving quill-driver's vengeance? But I forgive you nevertheless, because it is such eloquent witness to your great love for me. [Takes her in his arms.] And that is as it should be, my own darling Nora. Come what will, you may be sure I shall have both courage and strength if they be needed. You will see I am man enough to take everything upon myself.

NORA.

[in a horror-stricken voice]. What do you mean by that?

다시 불러들이세요! 그 편지가 우리에게 어떤 일을 초래할지 당신은 몰라요.

헬머

이미 늦었어.

노라

네, 이미 늦었어요.

헬머

그런 걱정을 하는 것이 나를 모욕하는 것이긴 하지만 용서하지. 내가 굶주린 하급 서기관의 복수를 두려워해야 한다니 모욕적이지 않아? 하지만 나를 향한 사랑에 대한 표현이니 당신을 용서하지. (노라를 껴안는다) 그리고 당연히 그렇게 해야 해. 사랑하는 노라.

무슨 일이 있어도 필요하다면 나는 용기와 힘, 둘 다 있다는 것을 믿어도 좋아. 내가 모든 것을 떠맡을 수 있는 사람이라는 걸 알게 될 거야.

노라

(공포에 떠는 목소리로) 그게 무슨 뜻이죠?

HELMER.

Everything, I say—

NORA.

[recovering herself]. You will never have to do that.

HELMER.

That's right. Well, we will share it, Nora, as man and wife should. That is how it shall be. [Caressing her.] Are you content now? There! There!—not these frightened dove's eyes! The whole thing is only the wildest fancy!— Now, you must go and play through the Tarantella and practise with your tambourine. I shall go into the inner office and shut the door, and I shall hear nothing; you can make as much noise as you please. [Turns back at the door.] And when Rank comes, tell him where he will find me. [Nods to her, takes his papers and goes into his room, and shuts the door after him.]practice

NORA.

[bewildered with anxiety, stands as if rooted to the spot, and whispers]. He was capable of doing it. He will do it. He will do it in spite of everything.—No, not that!

헬머

모두 책임지겠다고.

노라

(진정하며) 당신이 그렇게 해서는 안 돼요.

헬머

알았어. 좋아, 서로 분담하지, 노라. 남편과 아내로서 말이야. 그래야 하는 것이 당연하지. (노라를 애무하며) 이제 만족해? 자, 자! 놀란 비둘기 같은 눈으로 보지 마! 모두 엉뚱한 공상일 뿐이야! 이제 당신은 타란텔라 연습하고 탬버린 연습도 해야지. 난 서재로 들어가 문을 잠그겠어, 그러면 아무것도 안 들리지. 원하는 대로 소리 내도 좋아. (문에서 뒤돌아본다) 그리고 랑크가 오면 내가 있는 곳을 말해줘. (고개를 끄덕이고 서류를 챙겨 자신의 서재로 올라간다. 그리고 문을 닫는다)

노라

(걱정으로 혼란스러워하며 그 자리에서 굳어 버린 듯 서서. 혼자 중얼거린다) 그는 그렇게 할 수 있는 사람이었지. 그 일을 할 거야. 결국 할 거야. 안 돼, 그건 아니야!

Never, never! Anything rather than that! Oh, for some help, some way out of it! [The door-bell rings.] Doctor Rank! Anything rather than that—anything, whatever it is! [She puts her hands over her face, pulls herself together, goes to the door and opens it. RANK is standing without, hanging up his coat. During the following dialogue it begins to grow dark.]

NORA.

Good day, Doctor Rank. I knew your ring. But you mustn't go in to Torvald now; I think he is busy with something.

RANK.

And you?

NORA.

[brings him in and shuts the door after him]. Oh, you know very well I always have time for you.

RANK.

Thank you. I shall make use of as much of it as I can.

절대로, 절대로! 다른 어떤 일이 있어도! 도움을 받아 빠져나가야
해! (현관에서 벨이 울린다) 랑크 선생님이군! 다른 무슨 일이 있어도
그것만은! (손으로 얼굴을 매만지고 정신을 차려 현관으로 가서 문을 연다.
랑크는 코트를 걸치고 밖에 서 있다. 다음 대화부터 점점 어두워진다)

노라

안녕하세요. 랑크 선생님. 벨 소리로 알았지요. 그런데 지금 토르
발에게 가시면 안 돼요. 그이는 일하느라 바빠요.

랑크

그럼, 부인은요?

노라

(랑크를 안으로 들이고 문을 닫는다) 오, 선생님을 위해서라면 저는
항상 시간이 있다는 걸 아시잖아요.

랑크

고맙소. 그럼 할 수 있는 한 그 시간을 이용하겠소.

NORA.

What do you mean by that? As much of it as you can?

RANK.

Well, does that alarm you?

NORA.

It was such a strange way of putting it. Is anything likely to happen?

RANK.

Nothing but what I have long been prepared for. But I certainly didn't expect it to happen so soon.

NORA.

[gripping him by the arm]. What have you found out? Doctor Rank, you must tell me.

RANK.

[sitting down by the stove]. It is all up with me. And it can't be helped.

노라

그게 무슨 뜻이죠? 할 수 있는 한이라뇨?

랑크

오, 놀라셨소?

노라

표현이 이상해서요. 무슨 일 있으세요?

랑크

오래전부터 각오하고 있던 일인걸요. 그런데 이렇게 일찍 오리라 곤 생각지도 못했죠.

노라

(그의 팔을 잡으며) 무엇을 알아내셨죠? 랑크 선생님, 말씀 해주세요.

랑크

(난롯가에 앉으며) 모든 게 끝입니다. 어쩔 수가 없어요.

NORA.

[with a sigh of relief]. Is it about yourself?

RANK.

Who else? It is no use lying to one's self. I am the most wretched of all my patients, Mrs Helmer. Lately I have been taking stock of my internal economy. Bankrupt! Probably within a month I shall lie rotting in the churchyard.

NORA.

What an ugly thing to say!

RANK.

The thing itself is cursedly ugly, and the worst of it is that I shall have to face so much more that is ugly before that. I shall only make one more examination of myself; when I have done that, I shall know pretty certainly when it will be that the horrors of dissolution will begin. There is something I want to tell you. Helmer's refined nature gives him an unconquerable disgust at everything that is ugly; I won't have him in my sick-room.

노라

(안도의 한숨을 쉬며) 선생님 얘기인가요?

랑크

그럼 누구겠습니까? 스스로를 속여봤자 소용없어요. 제 환자 중에서 제가 가장 비참한 사람이오, 헬머 부인. 최근 제 몸을 살펴보았어요. 파멸이에요! 아마도 한 달 이내에 관에서 썩어갈 것이오.

노라

무슨 그런 험한 말씀을!

랑크

일 자체가 지독하게 추악하지요. 그리고 가장 나쁜 건 이전보다 추악한 것을 더 많이 거쳐야 한다는 겁니다. 마지막 검사만 하면 되는데 그게 끝나면 죽음의 공포가 언제 시작되는지 분명히 알게 됩니다. 부인에게 하고 싶은 말이 있어요. 헬머는 깔끔한 성격이라 모든 추한 일을 극도로 싫어하니 내 병실에는 들여보내지 말아 주세요.

NORA.

Oh, but, Doctor Rank—

RANK.

I won't have him there. Not on any account. I bar my door to him. As soon as I am quite certain that the worst has come, I shall send you my card with a black cross on it, and then you will know that the loathsome end has begun.

NORA.

You are quite absurd today. And I wanted you so much to be in a really good humour.

RANK.

With death stalking beside me?—To have to pay this penalty for another man's sin? Is there any justice in that? And in every single family, in one way or another, some such inexorable retribution is being exacted—

NORA.

[putting her hands over her ears]. Rubbish! Do talk of something cheerful.

노라

오, 하지만 랑크 선생님…….

랑크

그곳에서 그를 보지 않을 것이오. 어떤 이유가 있어도 안 됩니다. 방에 빗장을 지를 거예요. 최악의 상황이 확인되는 대로 내 명함에 검은 십자가를 그려 부인에게 보낼 겁니다. 그때가 끔찍한 최후가 시작되었다는 것을 알게 될 것이오.

노라

선생님, 오늘 정말 이상해요. 저는 선생님의 기분 좋은 모습을 보고 싶었는데.

랑크

죽음이 내 옆에 달라붙어 있는데도요? 다른 사람의 죄로 벌을 받아야 한다니요? 정의라는 게 있는 겁니까? 모든 가정마다 어떻게든 냉혹한 징벌이 일어나죠.

노라

(손으로 귀를 막고) 헛소리! 기운 나는 말씀을 하세요!

RANK.

Oh, it's a mere laughing matter, the whole thing. My poor innocent spine has to suffer for my father's youthful amusements.

NORA.

[sitting at the table on the left]. I suppose you mean that he was too partial to asparagus and pate de foie gras, don't you?

RANK.

Yes, and to truffles.

NORA.

Truffles, yes. And oysters too, I suppose?

RANK.

Oysters, of course, that goes without saying.

NORA.

And heaps of port and champagne. It is sad that all these nice things should take their revenge on our bones.

랑크

오, 이건 단지 우스운 일이오. 내 죄 없는 척추가 아버지의 젊은 시절 유흥 때문에 고통받아야 하오.

노라

(테이블 왼쪽에 앉으며) 아버님이 아스파라거스와 거위 간 요리를 아주 좋아하셨다면서요. 그렇죠?

랑크

네, 송로 버섯도요.

노라

송로 버섯, 그렇죠. 굴도 좋아하신 것 같은데, 그렇죠?

랑크

굴, 당연히, 그야 말할 것도 없죠.

노라

포도주와 샴페인도 말이죠. 이런 맛있는 것들이 우리 뼈를 해롭게 하다니 슬프군요.

RANK.

Especially that they should revenge themselves on the unlucky bones of those who have not had the satisfaction of enjoying them.

NORA.

Yes, that's the saddest part of it all.

RANK.

[with a searching look at her]. Hm!—

NORA.

[after a short pause]. Why did you smile?

RANK.

No, it was you that laughed.

NORA.

No, it was you that smiled, Doctor Rank!

RANK.

[rising]. You are a greater rascal than I thought.

랑크

특히나 그런 음식을 즐기지 않는 불행한 사람의 뼈에 해를 끼치다니요.

노라

그래요, 그게 가장 슬픈 일이죠.

랑크

(노라를 살펴보는 눈초리로) 음…….

노라

(잠시 멈추며) 왜 그렇게 웃으시죠?

랑크

아뇨, 웃은 건 부인이오.

노라

아니에요, 선생님이 웃으셨어, 랑크 선생님!

랑크

(일어서며) 부인은 내가 생각했던 것보다 훨씬 장난꾸러기요.

NORA.

I am in a silly mood today.

RANK.

So it seems.

NORA.

[putting her hands on his shoulders]. Dear, dear Doctor Rank, death mustn't take you away from Torvald and me.

RANK.

It is a loss you would easily recover from. Those who are gone are soon forgotten.

NORA.

[looking at him anxiously]. Do you believe that?

RANK.

People form new ties, and then—

NORA.

Who will form new ties?

노라

저는 오늘 좀 바보 같아요.

랑크

그런 것 같소.

노라

(손을 랑크 어깨에 얹고) 소중한 랑크 선생님, 죽음이 토르발과 저에게서 선생님을 데려갈 수 없어요.

랑크

쉽게 회복되는 것이 죽임이오. 떠난 사람들은 곧 잊히니까.

노라

(걱정스럽게 바라보며) 그렇게 믿으세요?

랑크

사람들은 새로운 인연을 맺고, 그러고 나면⋯⋯.

노라

누가 새로운 인연을 맺죠?

RANK.

Both you and Helmer, when I am gone. You yourself are already on the high road to it, I think. What did that Mrs Linde want here last night?

NORA.

Oho!—you don't mean to say you are jealous of poor Christine?

RANK.

Yes, I am. She will be my successor in this house. When I am done for, this woman will—

NORA.

Hush! don't speak so loud. She is in that room.

RANK.

Today again. There, you see.

NORA.

She has only come to sew my dress for me. Bless my soul, how unreasonable you are! [Sits down on the sofa.]

랑크

내가 가버리면 부인과 헬머 둘 다요. 부인은 벌써 그렇게 하는
것 같소. 지난밤 린데 부인이 여기에 무슨 일로 왔소?

노라

어머! 설마 가여운 린데 부인을 질투하시는 건 아니죠?

랑크

맞소, 질투합니다. 이 집에서 그 부인이 나를 대신할 것이오.
내가 없어지면, 그 부인이…….

노라

쉿! 큰 소리 내지 말아요. 린데 부인 저쪽 방에 있어요.

랑크

오늘도 왔군. 거봐요.

노라

린데 부인은 저를 위해 드레스 바느질하러 오신 것뿐이에요.
저런! 지나치세요! (소파에 앉는다)

Be nice now, Doctor Rank, and tomorrow you will see how beautifully I shall dance, and you can imagine I am doing it all for you—and for Torvald too, of course. [Takes various things out of the box.] Doctor Rank, come and sit down here, and I will show you something.

RANK.

[sitting down]. What is it?

NORA.

Just look at those!

RANK.

Silk stockings.

NORA.

Flesh-coloured. Aren't they lovely? It is so dark here now, but tomorrow—. No, no, no! you must only look at the feet. Oh well, you may have leave to look at the legs too.

RANK.

Hm!—

랑크 선생님, 내일이면 제가 얼마나 멋지게 춤출지 볼 수 있을 거예요. 선생님을 위해서 하는 거라고 생각하셔도 좋아요, 물론 토르발을 위해서도 말이죠. (상자에서 여러 가지 물건을 꺼낸다) 랑크 선생님, 여기 오셔서 앉아요. 보여드릴 게 있어요.

랑크

(앉으며) 그게 뭔데요?

노라

이것들 좀 보세요!

랑크

실크 스타킹이군요.

노라

살색이에요. 예쁘지 않나요? 지금 여기서는 너무 어둡지만 내일이면……. 아니, 안 돼요! 발만 보셔야 해요. 좋아요. 다리도 보여드리죠.

랑크

음!

NORA.

Why are you looking so critical? Don't you think they will fit me?

RANK.

I have no means of forming an opinion about that.

NORA.

[looks at him for a moment]. For shame! [Hits him lightly on the ear with the stockings.] That's to punish you. [Folds them up again.]

RANK.

And what other nice things am I to be allowed to see?

NORA.

Not a single thing more, for being so naughty. [She looks among the things, humming to herself.]

RANK.

[after a short silence]. When I am sitting here, talking to you as intimately as this, I cannot imagine for a moment what would have become of me if I had never come into this house.

노라

왜 그리 심각하게 보시죠? 저에게 어울리지 않는다고 생각하시나요?

랑크

이런 일에 의견을 말할 수 없소.

노라

(잠깐 랑크를 바라본다) **어머, 망측해라!** (스타킹으로 가볍게 랑크의 귀를 때린다) **이건 벌이예요.** (스타킹을 다시 접는다)

랑크

뭐 다른 예쁜 것들을 볼 수 있나요?

노라

더 이상은 안 돼요, 아주 무례했어요. (콧노래를 부르며 물건을 살핀다)

랑크

(잠시 침묵이 흐르고) 내가 여기에 앉아 부인과 친밀하게 대화하니 만약 이 집에 한 번도 오지 않았다면 내가 어떻게 되었을지 상상할 수 없군요.

NORA.

[smiling]. I believe you do feel thoroughly at home with us.

RANK.

[in a lower voice, looking straight in front of him]. And to be obliged to leave it all—

NORA.

Nonsense, you are not going to leave it.

RANK.

[as before]. And not be able to leave behind one the slightest token of one's gratitude, scarcely even a fleeting regret—nothing but an empty place which the first comer can fill as well as any other.

NORA.

And if I asked you now for a—? No!

RANK.

For what?

노라

(미소 지으며) 이 집에서 우리와 함께 있을 때 정말 편안하실 거라고 믿어요.

랑크

(낮은 목소리로 앞을 바라보며) 이제 다 두고 떠나야 한다니…….

노라

말도 안 돼요. 선생님은 떠나지 않을 거예요.

랑크

(계속 해서) 감사 표시로 변변찮은 것도 하나 남길 수 없다니요. 찰나의 후회조차 없이 처음 온 사람이 다른 사람들처럼 채울 수 있는 빈 곳만 있을 뿐입니다.

노라

만약 제가 부탁을 드린다면……? 아니에요!

랑크

무슨 부탁이오?

NORA.

For a big proof of your friendship—

RANK.

Yes, yes!

NORA.

I mean a tremendously big favour—

RANK.

Would you really make me so happy for once?

NORA.

Ah, but you don't know what it is yet.

RANK.

No—but tell me.

NORA.

I really can't, Doctor Rank. It is something out of all reason; it means advice, and help, and a favour—

노라

선생님의 우정을 입증할 만한 일······.

랑크

네, 좋아요!

노라

정말 큰 부탁인데요······.

랑크

이번에는 나를 행복하게 해주려는 거요?

노라

그런데 선생님은 그게 무엇인지 아직 모르시잖아요.

랑크

그렇긴 하지만, 이제 말해보시오.

노라

말할 수 없어요. 랑크 선생님, 그건 도리에 맞지 않은 일이에요. 충고나 도움뿐만 아니라 큰 호의가 따르는 일이거든요······.

RANK.

The bigger a thing it is the better. I can't conceive what it is you mean. Do tell me. Haven't I your confidence?

NORA.

More than anyone else. I know you are my truest and best friend, and so I will tell you what it is. Well, Doctor Rank, it is something you must help me to prevent. You know how devotedly, how inexpressibly deeply Torvald loves me; he would never for a moment hesitate to give his life for me.

RANK.

[leaning towards her]. Nora—do you think he is the only one—?

NORA.

[with a slight start]. The only one—?

RANK.

The only one who would gladly give his life for your sake.

랑크

큰 부탁일수록 좋소. 그게 뭔지 모르겠지만 말이오, 말해보시오. 나에 대한 신뢰가 없소?

노라

누구보다도 신뢰하지요. 선생님은 제게 둘도 없는 친구라는 걸 알아요, 그래서 선생님께 말씀드리려고 해요. 랑크 선생님, 저를 도와서 막아야 할 일이 있어요. 토르발이 헌신적으로, 표현할 수 없을 정도로 저를 깊이 사랑한다는 거 아시죠. 그이는 저를 위해서 목숨을 바치는 것을 결코 한순간도 망설이지 않을 거예요.

랑크

(노라에게 몸을 기울이며) 노라, 토르발만이 유일한 사람이라고 생각하오?

노라

(살짝 놀라며) 유일한 사람?

랑크

당신을 위해서 목숨을 기꺼이 바치려는 유일한 사람 말이오.

NORA.

[sadly]. Is that it?

RANK.

I was determined you should know it before I went away, and there will never be a better opportunity than this. Now you know it, Nora. And now you know, too, that you can trust me as you would trust no one else.

NORA.

[rises, deliberately and quietly]. Let me pass.

RANK.

[makes room for her to pass him, but sits still]. Nora!

NORA.

[at the hall door]. Helen, bring in the lamp. [Goes over to the stove.] Dear Doctor Rank, that was really horrid of you.

RANK.

To have loved you as much as anyone else does? Was that horrid?

노라

(구슬프게) 설마?

랑크

내가 떠나기 전에 당신이 알아야 한다고 결심했소. 이것보다 더 좋은 기회는 없을 거요. 이제 당신은 내 마음을 알아요, 노라. 이제 부인은 다른 누구보다도 나를 신뢰할 수 있다는 것도 아시죠.

노라

(찬찬히, 조용하게 일어선다) **지나갈게요.**

랑크

(지나가도록 비켜준다, 그러나 여전히 앉아있다) **노라!**

노라

(현관문 쪽으로) **헬렌, 램프를 가지고 와.** (난로 쪽으로 간다) 랑크 선생님, 그 말씀은 정말 **불쾌했어요.**

랑크

다른 사람들처럼 당신을 사랑하는 것이 **불쾌**하다고요?

NORA.

No, but to go and tell me so. There was really no need
—

RANK.

What do you mean? Did you know—? [MAID enters with lamp, puts it down on the table, and goes out.] Nora—Mrs Helmer—tell me, had you any idea of this?

NORA.

Oh, how do I know whether I had or whether I hadn't? I really can't tell you—To think you could be so clumsy, Doctor Rank! We were getting on so nicely.

RANK.

Well, at all events you know now that you can command me, body and soul. So won't you speak out?

NORA.

[looking at him]. After what happened?

RANK.

I beg you to let me know what it is.

노라

아뇨, 하지만 저에게 그렇게 말씀하시다니, 정말 그럴 필요가 없는데…….

랑크

그게 무슨 뜻이죠? 알았어요? (하녀가 램프를 가지고 들어와 테이블에 놓고 나간다) 노라, 헬머 부인, 말해요. 내 마음을 알고 있었죠?

노라

제가 알았든 몰랐든 어떻게 알겠어요? 말씀드릴 수 없어요. 생각해 보니 선생님은 정말 어설프군요. 랑크 선생님! 우리는 지금까지 잘 지내왔잖아요.

랑크

글쎄요, 어쨌든 부인은 이제 내 몸과 마음을 마음대로 할 수 있다는 것을 알고 있소. 그럼 그 얘기 하지 않겠소?

노라

(랑크를 바라보며) 일이 이렇게 됐는데도요?

랑크

그게 무슨 일인지 제발 알려주시오.

NORA.

I can't tell you anything now.

RANK.

Yes, yes. You mustn't punish me in that way. Let me have permission to do for you whatever a man may do.

NORA.

You can do nothing for me now. Besides, I really don't need any help at all. You will find that the whole thing is merely fancy on my part. It really is so—of course it is! [Sits down in the rocking-chair, and looks at him with a smile.] You are a nice sort of man, Doctor Rank!—don't you feel ashamed of yourself, now the lamp has come?

RANK.

Not a bit. But perhaps I had better go—for ever?

NORA.

No, indeed, you shall not. Of course you must come here just as before. You know very well Torvald can't do without you.

노라

이젠 어떤 것도 말할 수 없어요.

랑크

나를 그런 식으로 벌하지 마시오. 부인을 위해 무슨 일이든 하게 허락해 주시오.

노라

선생님은 이제 저를 위해 아무 일도 할 수 없어요. 게다가 아무 도움도 필요하지 않아요. 모든 것이 저에게는 단지 공상이라는 것을 알게 될 거예요. 정말 그래요, 당연하죠! (흔들의자에 앉아 랑크를 바라보며 미소 짓는다) 당신은 정말 좋은 사람이에요, 랑크 선생님! 램프가 켜지니 좀 창피하지 않으세요?

랑크

조금도요, 하지만 저는 가는 게 나을 것 같군요. 영원히 말이죠?

노라

아뇨, 정말 그래서는 안 돼요, 물론 예전처럼 여기 와주셔야 해요. 토르발이 당신 없이는 안된다는 것을 잘 아시잖아요.

277

RANK.

Yes, but you?

NORA.

Oh, I am always tremendously pleased when you come.

RANK.

It is just that, that put me on the wrong track. You are a riddle to me. I have often thought that you would almost as soon be in my company as in Helmer's.

NORA.

Yes—you see there are some people one loves best, and others whom one would almost always rather have as companions.

RANK.

Yes, there is something in that.

NORA.

When I was at home, of course I loved papa best. But I always thought it tremendous fun if I could steal down into the maids' room, because they never moralised at all, and talked to each other about such entertaining things.

랑크

알죠, 그런데 부인은?

노라

오, 선생님이 오시면 저는 항상 기뻐요.

랑크

바로 그 점이 나를 착각하게 했소. 부인은 내게 수수께끼 같소. 부인이 나와 같이 있는 것이 헬머와 함께 있는 것만큼이나 좋아하는 것이라고 종종 생각했소.

노라

그래요, 가장 사랑하는 사람도 있고 친구로 삼고 싶어 하는 사람도 있으니까요.

랑크

네, 그 말에 일리가 있네요.

노라

어렸을 때, 물론 아빠를 가장 사랑했어요. 하지만 하녀들 방에 몰래 들어가는 것도 정말 즐거웠지요. 하녀들은 저를 절대 나무라지 않았고 서로 재미있는 이야기를 나누었으니까요.

RANK.

I see—it is their place I have taken.

NORA.

[jumping up and going to him]. Oh, dear, nice Doctor Rank, I never meant that at all. But surely you can understand that being with Torvald is a little like being with papa—[Enter MAID from the hall.]

MAID.

If you please, ma'am. [Whispers and hands her a card.]

NORA.

[glancing at the card]. Oh! [Puts it in her pocket.]

RANK.

Is there anything wrong?

NORA.

No, no, not in the least. It is only something—it is my new dress—

랑크

알겠네요, 제가 하녀 대신이군요.

노라

(벌떡 일어나 랑크에게 간다) 어머나, 우리 랑크 선생님, 그런 뜻으로 한 말이 아니에요. 하지만 토르발과 함께 있으면 마치 아버지와 함께 있는 것 같다는 것을 이해하실 거예요. (현관에서 하녀가 들어온다)

하녀

저기, 마님. (속삭이며 노라에게 명함 한 장을 건넨다)

노라

(명함을 힐끗 보며) 하! (주머니 속에 명함을 넣는다)

랑크

무슨 잘못된 일이라도 있나요?

노라

아뇨, 아뇨, 전혀요. 사소한 일이에요. 이건 제 드레스⋯⋯.

RANK.

What? Your dress is lying there.

NORA.

Oh, yes, that one; but this is another. I ordered it. Torvald mustn't know about it—

RANK.

Oho! Then that was the great secret.

NORA.

Of course. Just go in to him; he is sitting in the inner room. Keep him as long as—

RANK.

Make your mind easy; I won't let him escape.

[Goes into HELMER'S room.]

NORA.

[to the MAID]. And he is standing waiting in the kitchen?

랑크

네? 당신 드레스는 저기 있는데요.

노라

네, 맞아요. 하지만 저건 다른 거예요. 제가 주문했어요. 토르발이 알면 안 돼요.

랑크

오! 그럼 큰 비밀이었군요.

노라

당연하죠. 토르발에게 가보세요, 서재에 있어요. 그리고 될 수 있는 한 그를 오래 붙잡아 두세요.

랑크

마음 편히 계세요. 도망가지 못하게 할 테니까요.

(헬머 방으로 들어간다)

노라

(하녀에게) 그 사람, 부엌에서 기다리고 있니?

MAID.

Yes; he came up the back stairs.

NORA.

But didn't you tell him no one was in?

MAID.

Yes, but it was no good.

NORA.

He won't go away?

MAID.

No; he says he won't until he has seen you, ma'am.

NORA.

Well, let him come in—but quietly. Helen, you mustn't say anything about it to anyone. It is a surprise for my husband.

MAID.

Yes, ma'am, I quite understand. [Exit.]

하녀

네, 뒷계단으로 올라오셨어요.

노라

그런데 아무도 없다고 말하지 않았어?

하녀

말씀드렸지만, 소용이 없었어요.

노라

가지 않으려고 했니?

하녀

네, 마님을 뵙기 전에는 가지 않겠다고 하세요.

노라

그럼, 들여보내. 하지만 아무도 모르게 말이야. 헬렌, 아무에게도
이 일을 말해서는 안 돼. 남편이 알면 놀라니까.

하녀

네, 마님 알겠습니다. (퇴장)

NORA.

This dreadful thing is going to happen! It will happen in spite of me! No, no, no, it can't happen—it shan't happen! [She bolts the door of HELMER'S room. The MAID opens the hall door for KROGSTAD and shuts it after him. He is wearing a fur coat, high boots and a fur cap.]

NORA.

[advancing towards him]. Speak low—my husband is at home.

KROGSTAD.

No matter about that.

NORA.

What do you want of me?

KROGSTAD.

An explanation of something.

NORA.

Make haste then. What is it?

노라

두려운 일이 일어나고 있어! 어쩔 수 없나 봐! 아니야, 안 돼, 그럴 수 없어, 그래선 안 돼! (노라는 헬머 방문을 잠근다. 하녀가 현관문을 열어 크로그스터를 들인 후 문을 닫는다. 그는 모피코트를 입고 장화를 신고 있으며 모피 모자를 쓰고 있다)

노라

(그에게 다가가며) 목소리 낮춰주세요. 남편이 집에 있어요.

크로그스터

상관없습니다.

노라

제게 원하는 게 뭐죠?

크로그스터

설명이오.

노라

그럼, 빨리 말하세요. 무슨 설명이죠?

KROGSTAD.

You know, I suppose, that I have got my dismissal.

NORA.

I couldn't prevent it, Mr. Krogstad. I fought as hard as I could on your side, but it was no good.

KROGSTAD.

Does your husband love you so little, then? He knows what I can expose you to, and yet he ventures—

NORA.

How can you suppose that he has any knowledge of the sort?

KROGSTAD.

I didn't suppose so at all. It would not be the least like our dear Torvald Helmer to show so much courage—

NORA.

Mr. Krogstad, a little respect for my husband, please.

크로그스터

아시다시피, 나는 해고 통지서를 받았어요.

노라

막을 수가 없었어요, 크로그스터 씨. 당신 편에서 최선을 다해 싸웠지만 소용이 없었어요.

크로그스터

그럼, 남편께선 부인을 별로 사랑하지 않나요? 내가 부인이 한 짓을 폭로할 수 있다는 것을 알면서 감히 …….

노라

남편이 이 일을 안다고 생각하시나요?

크로그스터

전혀 아니지요. 우리 친애하는 토르발 헬머가 많은 용기를 보여 줄 것 같지 않거든요.

노라

크로그스터 씨, 남편을 존중해 주세요.

KROGSTAD.

Certainly—all the respect he deserves. But since you have kept the matter so carefully to yourself, I make bold to suppose that you have a little clearer idea, than you had yesterday, of what it actually is that you have done?

NORA.

More than you could ever teach me.

KROGSTAD.

Yes, such a bad lawyer as I am.

NORA.

What is it you want of me?

KROGSTAD.

Only to see how you were, Mrs Helmer. I have been thinking about you all day long. A mere cashier, a quill-driver, a—well, a man like me—even he has a little of what is called feeling, you know.

크로그스터

물론, 그는 존경받아 마땅하오. 그러나 부인이 그 문제를 조심스럽게 혼자만 아시니 부인께서 저질렀던 일이 실제로 어떤 것인지 어제보다 더 명확하게 아실 거라고 감히 생각해도 되겠습니까?

노라

당신이 저를 가르치려는 것보다 더 잘 압니다.

크로그스터

좋소, 나는 형편없는 변호사니까요.

노라

저에게 원하는 게 뭐죠?

크로그스터

부인이 어떻게 지냈는지 보러 왔습니다. 하루 종일 부인에 대해 생각했어요. 단지 말단 은행원이지만 저 같은 사람도 감정이라는 게 있습니다.

NORA.

Show it, then; think of my little children.

KROGSTAD.

Have you and your husband thought of mine? But never mind about that. I only wanted to tell you that you need not take this matter too seriously. In the first place there will be no accusation made on my part.

NORA.

No, of course not; I was sure of that.

KROGSTAD.

The whole thing can be arranged amicably; there is no reason why anyone should know anything about it. It will remain a secret between us three.

NORA.

My husband must never get to know anything about it.

KROGSTAD.

How will you be able to prevent it? Am I to understand that you can pay the balance that is owing?

노라

그럼, 보여주세요. 제 어린아이들을 생각해 주세요.

크로그스터

부인과 남편은 내 아이들을 생각해 주셨나요? 하지만 그건 신경
쓰지 마세요. 나는 부인이 이 문제를 너무 심각하게 여길 필요가
없다는 것을 말하고 싶었을 뿐입니다. 우선 내 입장에서 고소하지
는 않을 것입니다.

노라

네, 당연히 그러셔야죠. 그러실 거라 믿었어요.

크로그스터

모든 것이 원만하게 정리될 수 있어요. 아무도 이에 대해 알 필
요가 없고요. 우리 세 사람 사이의 비밀로 남게 될 겁니다.

노라

남편이 이 일을 절대 알아서는 안 돼요.

크로그스터

부인께서 어떻게 막을 수 있나요? 나머지 돈을 갚을 수 있다는
뜻입니까?

NORA.

No, not just at present.

KROGSTAD.

Or perhaps that you have some expedient for raising the money soon?

NORA.

No expedient that I mean to make use of.

KROGSTAD.

Well, in any case, it would have been of no use to you now. If you stood there with ever so much money in your hand, I would never part with your bond.

NORA.

Tell me what purpose you mean to put it to.

KROGSTAD.

I shall only preserve it—keep it in my possession. No one who is not concerned in the matter shall have the slightest hint of it. So that if the thought of it has driven you to any desperate resolution—

노라

아뇨, 현재로서는 안 돼요.

크로그스터

그러면 곧 돈을 마련할 방법은 있습니까?

노라

별다른 방법은 없어요.

크로그스터

뭐, 어쨌든 그런 것은 이제 아무 소용이 없어요. 부인 손에 많은 돈이 있다 하더라도 차용증서는 내주지 않을 것이니까요.

노라

그걸 가지고 어쩔 작정이죠?

크로그스터

단지 보관할 것입니다. 내 수중에 두고요. 이 일과 관련되지 않은 사람은 전혀 모를 거요. 만약 그것 때문에 부인이 무모한 결심을 하게 된다면……

NORA.

It has.

KROGSTAD.

If you had it in your mind to run away from your home—

NORA.

I had.

KROGSTAD.

Or even something worse—

NORA.

How could you know that?

KROGSTAD.

Give up the idea.

NORA.

How did you know I had thought of that?

노라

실제로 그래요.

크로그스터

만약 집을 나가버리는 생각을 한다거나……

노라

그런 생각 했어요.

크로그스터

또는 최악의 상황으로…….

노라

어떻게 그걸 아시죠?

크로그스터

그런 생각은 하지 마세요.

노라

제가 그런 생각을 했다는 것을 어떻게 아셨죠?

KROGSTAD.

Most of us think of that at first. I did, too—but I hadn't the courage.

NORA.

[faintly]. No more had I.

KROGSTAD.

[in a tone of relief]. No, that's it, isn't it—you hadn't the courage either?

NORA.

No, I haven't—I haven't.

KROGSTAD.

Besides, it would have been a great piece of folly. Once the first storm at home is over—. I have a letter for your husband in my pocket.

NORA.

Telling him everything?

크로그스터

대부분 사람이 처음에는 그런 일을 생각하죠. 저도 그랬으니까요. 하지만 용기가 없었소.

노라

(힘없이) 저도 없어요.

크로그스터

(안심하는 말투로) 그렇죠. 바로 그거예요. 부인 역시 용기가 없죠?

노라

네, 없어요, 없어.

크로그스터

더군다나, 그것은 매우 어리석은 일이었을 것이오. 가정에 한차례 폭풍이 끝나면······. 내 주머니에 부인 남편에게 보낼 편지가 있소.

노라

그이에게 다 알릴 건가요?

KROGSTAD.

In as lenient a manner as I possibly could.

NORA.

[quickly]. He mustn't get the letter. Tear it up. I will find some means of getting money.

KROGSTAD.

Excuse me, Mrs Helmer, but I think I told you just now —

NORA.

I am not speaking of what I owe you. Tell me what sum you are asking my husband for, and I will get the money.

KROGSTAD.

I am not asking your husband for a penny.

NORA.

What do you want, then?

크로그스터

할 수 있는 한 부드럽게 쓰긴 했소.

노라

(재빠르게) 그가 편지를 받아서는 안 돼요. 찢어버리세요. 제가 어떻게 해서라도 돈을 마련할게요.

크로그스터

미안합니다만 헬머 부인, 방금 말씀드린 것 같은데요…….

노라

제가 빌린 돈을 말하는 게 아니에요. 남편에게 얼마의 돈을 요구하는지 말해보세요. 제가 드릴게요.

크로그스터

나는 부인 남편에게 푼돈을 요구하는 것이 아닙니다.

노라

그럼 뭘 원하시죠?

KROGSTAD.

I will tell you. I want to rehabilitate myself, Mrs Helmer; I want to get on; and in that your husband must help me. For the last year and a half I have not had a hand in anything dishonourable, amid all that time I have been struggling in most restricted circumstances. I was content to work my way up step by step. Now I am turned out, and I am not going to be satisfied with merely being taken into favour again. I want to get on, I tell you. I want to get into the Bank again, in a higher position. Your husband must make a place for me—

NORA.

That he will never do!

KROGSTAD.

He will; I know him; he dare not protest. And as soon as I am in there again with him, then you will see! Within a year I shall be the manager's right hand. It will be Nils Krogstad and not Torvald Helmer who manages the Bank.

크로그스터

말씀드리죠. 나는 명예를 회복하고 싶소, 헬머 부인. 나는 성공하고 싶소. 그래서 당신 남편이 나를 도와야 하오. 지난 일 년 반 동안 수치스러운 어떤 일에도 관여하지 않았고 그 시간 내내 가장 어려운 상황에서 고군분투하며 지냈소. 나는 차근차근 승진하는 데 만족했소. 이제는 쫓겨나게 되었으니 다시 인정받는 것에만 만족하지 않을 것이오. 난 정말로 성공하고 싶소. 다시 은행에 들어가 더 높은 직위에 오르고 싶소. 당신 남편이 내 자리를 마련해야 하오.

노라

그이는 절대 그런 일을 하지 않아요!

크로그스터

그는 할 겁니다. 그 사람을 잘 알죠. 반대할 용기가 없으니까요. 당신 남편과 같이 은행에 다니게 되면 일 년도 안 돼 나는 은행장의 오른팔이 된다는 것을 보게 될 겁니다! 은행을 관리하는 사람은 닐스 크로그스터이지 토르발 헬머가 아닙니다.

NORA.

That's a thing you will never see!

KROGSTAD.

Do you mean that you will—?

NORA.

I have courage enough for it now.

KROGSTAD.

Oh, you can't frighten me. A fine, spoilt lady like you—

NORA.

You will see, you will see.

KROGSTAD.

Under the ice, perhaps? Down into the cold, coal-black water? And then, in the spring, to float up to the surface, all horrible and unrecognisable, with your hair fallen out—

NORA.

You can't frighten me.

노라

그런 일은 절대 일어나지 않아요!

크로그스터

그렇다면 부인은?

노라

전 이제 각오했어요.

크로그스터

오, 부인은 나를 두렵게 할 수 없소. 당신처럼 곱게 자란 철부지 같은 여자가 …….

노라

두고 보세요, 두고 보시라고요!

크로그스터

얼음장 밑으로 들어가려고요? 차갑고 새까만 물속으로? 그럼 봄이 되면 끔찍하고 누군지 분간할 수 없는 모습으로 머리카락은 빠진 채 둥둥 떠오르게 될 겁니다.

노라

겁줘도 소용없어요.

KROGSTAD.

Nor you me. People don't do such things, Mrs Helmer. Besides, what use would it be? I should have him completely in my power all the same.

NORA.

Afterwards? When I am no longer—

KROGSTAD.

Have you forgotten that it is I who have the keeping of your reputation? [NORA stands speechlessly looking at him.] Well, now, I have warned you. Do not do anything foolish. When Helmer has had my letter, I shall expect a message from him. And be sure you remember that it is your husband himself who has forced me into such ways as this again. I will never forgive him for that. Goodbye, Mrs Helmer. [Exit through the hall.]

NORA.

[goes to the hall door, opens it slightly and listens.] He is going. He is not putting the letter in the box. Oh no, no! that's impossible! [Opens the door by degrees.] What is that? He is standing outside.

크로그스터

당신도 마찬가지요. 사람들은 이런 일들을 하지 않아요, 헬머 부인. 게다가 그게 무슨 소용 있소? 그래도 나는 그를 완벽히 내 손안에 두게 할 것이오.

노라

제가 사라져 버린 그 후에는요?

크로그스터

부인의 **평판**을 쥐고 있는 사람이 나라는 것을 잊었소? (노라는 말 없이 그를 바라보며 서 있다) 자, 이제 경고합니다. 어리석은 짓은 하지 마시오. 헬머가 내 편지를 읽으면, 나는 그에게서 답장을 받게 되겠죠. 제가 다시 이런 일을 하게 한 사람은 당신 남편 때문이었다는 것을 부인은 기억하게 될 것입니다. 이번 일은 그를 절대 용서할 수 없군요. 안녕히 계시오, 헬머 부인. (현관을 지나서 나간다)

노라

(현관문으로 가서 문을 살짝 열며 귀를 기울인다) 가고 있어. 우편함에 **편지**를 넣지 않네. 아, 안 돼! 그건 **불가능해!** (문을 조금 더 연다) 뭐지? 밖에 서 있잖아.

He is not going downstairs. Is he hesitating? Can he—? [A letter drops into the box; then KROGSTAD'S footsteps are heard, until they die away as he goes downstairs. NORA utters a stifled cry, and runs across the room to the table by the sofa. A short pause.]

NORA.

In the letter-box. [Steals across to the hall door.] There it lies—Torvald, Torvald, there is no hope for us now!

[Mrs Linde comes in from the room on the left, carrying the dress.]

MRS LINDE.

There, I can't see anything more to mend now. Would you like to try it on—?

NORA.

[in a hoarse whisper]. Christine, come here.

MRS LINDE.

[throwing the dress down on the sofa]. What is the matter with you? You look so agitated!

계단에 내려가지 않네. 주저하나? 만약 그렇다면? (편지가 우편함에 떨어지고 계단으로 내려가는 크로그스터의 발걸음 소리가 점점 작아진다. 노라는 낮게 비명을 지른다. 그리고 방을 가로질러 소파 옆 테이블로 달려간다. 잠시 후)

노라

우편함 속에 (현관문 쪽으로 살며시 가로질러 간다) 저기 편지가 있어. 토르발, 이제 우리에겐 희망이 없어요!

(린데 부인이 왼쪽 방에서 드레스를 들고나온다)

린데 부인

자, 이제 더 이상 손볼 곳은 없어. 한번 입어 볼래?

노라

(쉰 목소리로 낮게 말한다) 크리스티네, 이리로 좀 와 봐.

린데 부인

(소파에 드레스를 던지며) 무슨 일이야? 너 정말 불안해 보여!

NORA.

Come here. Do you see that letter? There, look—you can see it through the glass in the letter-box.

MRS LINDE.

Yes, I see it.

NORA.

That letter is from Krogstad.

MRS LINDE.

Nora—it was Krogstad who lent you the money!

NORA.

Yes, and now Torvald will know all about it.

MRS LINDE.

Believe me, Nora, that's the best thing for both of you.

NORA.

You don't know all. I forged a name.

노라

이쪽으로 와 봐. 저 편지 보이니? 저기 봐봐. 우편함 유리 속에 편지 보일 거야.

린데 부인

응, 보여.

노라

크로그스터가 보낸 편지야.

린데 부인

노라······ 돈을 크로그스터에게서 빌렸니?

노라

응, 그리고 이제 토르발이 모두 알게 될 거야.

린데 부인

노라, 두 사람에게 오히려 좋은 일이 될 거야.

노라

넌 아무것도 몰라. 내가 허위 서명했어.

MRS LINDE.

Good heavens—!

NORA.

I only want to say this to you, Christine—you must be my witness.

MRS LINDE.

Your witness? What do you mean? What am I to—?

NORA.

If I should go out of my mind—and it might easily happen—

MRS LINDE.

Nora!

NORA.

Or if anything else should happen to me—anything, for instance, that might prevent my being here—

MRS LINDE.

Nora! Nora! you are quite out of your mind.

린데 부인

맙소사!

노라

너에게 이 말만 하고 싶어, 크리스티네……. 내 증인이 되어줘.

린데 부인

너의 증인? 무슨 말이니? 내가 무엇을 해야 ……?

노라

만약 내가 미치기라도 하면, 그런 일이 일어날지도 몰라…….

린데 부인

노라!

노라

아니면 내게 다른 일이 생긴다면, 예를 들어 여기 있기 힘들게 되면…….

린데 부인

노라! 너 정말 정신 나갔구나!

NORA.

And if it should happen that there were some one who wanted to take all the responsibility, all the blame, you understand—

MRS LINDE.

Yes, yes—but how can you suppose—?

NORA.

Then you must be my witness, that it is not true, Christine. I am not out of my mind at all; I am in my right senses now, and I tell you no one else has known anything about it; I, and I alone, did the whole thing. Remember that.

MRS LINDE.

I will, indeed. But I don't understand all this.

NORA.

How should you understand it? A wonderful thing is going to happen!

노라

그리고 만약 모든 책임과 비난을 떠맡으려고 하는 사람이 있다면, 알겠지…….

린데 부인

그래, 그래……. 그런데 어떻게 그런 생각을 할 수 있니?

노라

그때 내 증인이 돼야 해, 그건 사실이 아니라고 말이야, 크리스티네. 나는 조금도 정신 나가지 않았어. 지금 정신 말짱해. 그리고 네에게 말하는데 아무도 이에 대해 아는 사람은 없어. 모두 나 혼자 한 일이야. 이 말 기억해 둬.

린데 부인

꼭 기억할게. 그런데 도무지 이해할 수가 없구나.

노라

네가 어떻게 이해하겠니? 놀라운 일이 곧 일어날 거야!

MRS LINDE.

A wonderful thing?

NORA.

Yes, a wonderful thing!—But it is so terrible, Christine; it mustn't happen, not for all the world.

MRS LINDE.

I will go at once and see Krogstad.

NORA.

Don't go to him; he will do you some harm.

MRS LINDE.

There was a time when he would gladly do anything for my sake.

NORA.

He?

MRS LINDE.

Where does he live?

린데 부인

놀라운 일?

노라

그래, 놀라운 일! 하지만 너무 무서운 일이야, 크리스티네.
무슨 일이 있어도 일어나서는 안 돼.

린데 부인

내가 당장 가서 크로그스터 씨를 만나보겠어.

노라

그 사람에게 가지 마. 너를 해코지할 거야.

린데 부인

그 남자는 나를 위해서 기꺼이 무슨 일이든 해주던 때가 있었어.

노라

그 사람이?

린데 부인

그가 어디에 살고 있니?

NORA.

How should I know—? Yes [feeling in her pocket], here is his card. But the letter, the letter—!

HELMER.

[calls from his room, knocking at the door]. Nora!

NORA.

[cries out anxiously]. Oh, what's that? What do you want?

HELMER.

Don't be so frightened. We are not coming in; you have locked the door. Are you trying on your dress?

NORA.

Yes, that's it. I look so nice, Torvald.

MRS LINDE.

[who has read the card]. I see he lives at the corner here.

노라

내가 어떻게 알겠니? 아 (주머니를 뒤진다), 여기 그의 명함이 있
어. 그런데 저 편지, 저 편지는 ……!

헬머

(문을 두드리며 서재에서 부른다) 노라!

노라

(불안하게 소리 지른다) 어머, 무슨 일이세요? 뭐가 필요해요?

헬머

그렇게 놀라지 마. 우리가 들어갈 수 없잖아. 문을 잠갔나 보군.
드레스 입고 있어?

노라

네, 입고 있어요. 정말 예뻐요, 토르발.

린데 부인

(명함을 보고) 그 사람은 저기 모퉁이에 살고 있군.

NORA.

Yes, but it's no use. It is hopeless. The letter is lying there in the box.

MRS LINDE.

And your husband keeps the key?

NORA.

Yes, always.

MRS LINDE.

Krogstad must ask for his letter back unread, he must find some pretence—

NORA.

But it is just at this time that Torvald generally—

MRS LINDE.

You must delay him. Go in to him in the meantime. I will come back as soon as I can. [She goes out hurriedly through the hall door.]

노라

맞아, 하지만 소용없어. 어쩔 수가 없어. 편지가 우편함에 있는 걸.

린데 부인

그럼, 남편이 열쇠를 가지고 있니?

노라

응, 항상.

린데 부인

크로그스터 씨는 동봉된 편지를 회수해야 해, 어떤 핑계를 만들어서라도 말이야.

노라

하지만 토르발이 보통 이 시간에…….

린데 부인

그를 붙잡고 있어. 잠시 동안 남편에게 가 있어. 최대한 빨리 돌아올게. (현관문을 통해 급히 밖으로 나간다)

NORA.

[goes to HELMER'S door, opens it and peeps in]. Torvald!

HELMER.

[from the inner room]. Well? May I venture at last to come into my own room again? Come along, Rank, now you will see— [Halting in the doorway.] But what is this?

NORA.

What is what, dear?

HELMER.

Rank led me to expect a splendid transformation.

RANK.

[in the doorway]. I understood so, but evidently I was mistaken.

NORA.

Yes, nobody is to have the chance of admiring me in my dress until tomorrow.

노라

(헬머 방으로 가서 문을 열고 안을 들여다본다) **토르발!**

헬머

(방안에서) 어이? 이제 내방으로 다시 들어가도 될까? 따라오시오, 랑크, 지금 볼 수 있을 것이오. (문 앞에서 멈추며) 아니, 이게 뭐야?

노라

왜요, 여보?

헬머

랑크는 멋지게 변신한 모습을 기대하라고 했는데.

랑크

(문 앞에서) 나도 그렇게 알았는데, 아마 착각했나 보오.

노라

음, 내일까지는 드레스 입은 저의 멋진 모습을 아무도 볼 수 없어요.

HELMER.

But, my dear Nora, you look so worn out. Have you been practising too much?

NORA.

No, I have not practised at all.

HELMER.

But you will need to—

NORA.

Yes, indeed I shall, Torvald. But I can't get on a bit without you to help me; I have absolutely forgotten the whole thing.

HELMER.

Oh, we will soon work it up again.

NORA.

Yes, help me, Torvald. Promise that you will! I am so nervous about it—all the people—. You must give yourself up to me entirely this evening. Not the tiniest bit of business—you mustn't even take a pen in your hand. Will you promise, Torvald dear?

헬머

그런데, 여보 노라, 당신 너무 지쳐 보여. 연습을 너무 많이 했나?

노라

아뇨, 전혀 연습하지 않았어요.

헬머

하지만 연습해야지.

노라

네, 해야죠. 토르발, 그런데 당신이 도와주지 않으면 전 조금도 잘 해낼 수 없어요. 전부 다 잊어버렸거든요.

헬머

오, 우리 둘이 하면 곧 생각날 거야.

노라

네, 도와주세요, 토르발. 약속해 줘요! 전 정말 떨려요. 많은 사람 앞에서……. 오늘 저녁은 오로지 저와 함께 있어야 해요. 아주 사소한 일도 하면 안 돼요. 손에 펜도 잡지 말고요. 약속해 주세요. 토르발?

HELMER.

I promise. This evening I will be wholly and absolutely at your service, you helpless little mortal. Ah, by the way, first of all I will just— [Goes towards the hall door.]

NORA.

What are you going to do there?

HELMER.

Only see if any letters have come.

NORA.

No, no! don't do that, Torvald!

HELMER.

Why not?

NORA.

Torvald, please don't. There is nothing there.

HELMER.

Well, let me look. [Turns to go to the letter-box. NORA, at the piano, plays the first bars of the Tarantella. HELMER stops in the doorway.] Aha!

헬머

약속하지. 오늘 저녁은 온전히 당신에게 바치겠소. 당신은 스스로 할 수 없는 사람이지. 오, 그나저나 우선은 …….(현관문 쪽으로 간다)

노라

저기에 뭐 하러 가시는 거죠?

헬머

편지가 왔는지 확인 좀 하려고.

노라

안 돼요! 가지 마세요. 토르발!

헬머

왜 그러는데?

노라

토르발, 제발 가지 마세요. 거기 아무것도 없어요.

헬머

글쎄, 보고 올게. (편지함으로 가려고 뒤돌아선다. 노라는 피아노로 타란텔라 곡의 첫 마디를 연주한다. 헬머가 문 앞에서 멈춰 선다) **아하!**

NORA.

I can't dance tomorrow if I don't practise with you.

HELMER.

[going up to her]. Are you really so afraid of it, dear?

NORA.

Yes, so dreadfully afraid of it. Let me practise at once; there is time now, before we go to dinner. Sit down and play for me, Torvald dear; criticise me, and correct me as you play.

HELMER.

With great pleasure, if you wish me to. [Sits down at the piano.]

NORA.

[takes out of the box a tambourine and a long variegated shawl. She hastily drapes the shawl round her. Then she springs to the front of the stage and calls out]. Now play for me! I am going to dance!

노라

당신과 함께 연습하지 않으면 저는 내일 춤을 출 수 없어요.

헬머

(노라에게 다가가며) 정말 그게 걱정돼, 여보?

노라

네, 너무나 걱정이 돼요. 당장 연습해요. 저녁 식사 전까지 시간이 있어요. 앉아서 반주를 해주세요, 토르발. 반주하면서 틀린 게 있으면 고쳐주세요.

헬머

당신이 원한다면 기꺼이. (피아노 앞에 앉는다)

노라

(상자에서 탬버린과 얼룩덜룩한 솔을 꺼낸다. 급히 몸에 걸치고 앞으로 튀어나와 소리친다) 자, 반주하세요! 춤추겠어요!

[HELMER plays and NORA dances. RANK stands by the piano behind HELMER, and looks on.]

HELMER.

[as he plays]. Slower, slower!

NORA.

I can't do it any other way.

HELMER.

Not so violently, Nora!

NORA.

This is the way.

HELMER.

[stops playing]. No, no—that is not a bit right.

NORA.

[laughing and swinging the tambourine]. Didn't I tell you so?

(헬머가 피아노 연주를 하고 노라는 춤을 춘다. 랑크는 헬머 뒤로 피아노 옆에 서서 구경한다)

헬머

(반주하면서) **천천히, 더 천천히!**

노라

다르게 할 수 없어요.

헬머

너무 격렬하게 추지마, 노라!

노라

이게 맞아요.

헬머

(반주를 멈추며) 아니야, 아니야, 조금도 맞지 않아.

노라

(웃으며 탬버린을 흔든다) 제가 그렇다고 말하지 않았나요?

RANK.

Let me play for her.

HELMER.

[getting up]. Yes, do. I can correct her better then.

[RANK sits down at the piano and plays. NORA dances more and more wildly. HELMER has taken up a position beside the stove, and during her dance gives her frequent instructions. She does not seem to hear him; her hair comes down and falls over her shoulders; she pays no attention to it, but goes on dancing. Enter Mrs Linde.]

MRS LINDE.

[standing as if spell-bound in the doorway]. Oh!—

NORA.

[as she dances]. Such fun, Christine!

HELMER.

My dear darling Nora, you are dancing as if your life depended on it.

랑크

내가 연주하겠네.

헬머

(일어서며) 그래, 좋아. 그러면 내가 더 잘 가르칠 수 있지.

(랑크가 피아노 앞에 앉아 연주한다. 노라는 점점 격하게 춤을 춘다. 헬머가 난로 옆에 자리 잡고 노라가 춤추는 동안 계속 지적한다. 노라는 그의 말이 들리지 않는 것 같다. 머리카락이 풀어져 어깨 위에 늘어졌지만, 신경 쓰지 않고 계속 춤을 춘다. 린데 부인이 들어온다)

린데 부인

(현관문에서 넋을 잃은 듯이 서 있다) 세상에!

노라

(춤추면서) 너무 재밌어, 크리스티네!

헬머

여보 노라, 당신 목숨 걸고 춤추는 것 같아.

NORA.

So it does.

HELMER.

Stop, Rank; this is sheer madness. Stop, I tell you! [RANK stops playing, and NORA suddenly stands still. HELMER goes up to her.] I could never have believed it. You have forgotten everything I taught you.

NORA.

[throwing away the tambourine]. There, you see.

HELMER.

You will want a lot of coaching.

NORA.

Yes, you see how much I need it. You must coach me up to the last minute. Promise me that, Torvald!

HELMER.

You can depend on me.

노라

맞아요.

헬머

그만, 랑크. 이거 완전히 미친 짓이야. 그만하라니까! (랑크는 연주를 멈추고 노라는 갑자기 서 있는다. 헬머가 노라에게 다가간다) **이럴 거라고 결코 생각하지 못했어. 내가 가르쳐준 것 모두 잊어버렸군.**

노라

(탬버린을 던지며) **보시다시피요.**

헬머

지도 많이 받아야겠는데.

노라

그러니, 제가 얼마나 도움이 필요한지 아셨죠. 끝까지 저를 가르쳐주셔야 해요. 그러겠다고 약속해요, 토르발!

헬머

안심해도 좋아.

NORA.

You must not think of anything but me, either today or tomorrow; you mustn't open a single letter—not even open the letter-box—

HELMER.

Ah, you are still afraid of that fellow—

NORA.

Yes, indeed I am.

HELMER.

Nora, I can tell from your looks that there is a letter from him lying there.

NORA.

I don't know; I think there is; but you must not read anything of that kind now. Nothing horrid must come between us until this is all over.

RANK.

[whispers to HELMER]. You mustn't contradict her.

노라

오늘도 내일도 저 이외에는 아무것도 생각하지 말아요. 편지 한 통도 뜯어서는 안 돼요. 편지함 열어보지도 말아요.

헬머

흠, 아직도 그놈을 두려워하는군.

노라

네, 두려워요.

헬머

노라, 당신 표정으로 알 수 있어. 저기에 그 사람이 보낸 편지가 있다고.

노라

모르겠어요. 있는 것 같기도 해요. 하지만 지금 그런 것 읽으면 안 돼요. 모든 것이 끝날 때까지 우리 사이에 어떤 불쾌한 일이 들어와서는 안 돼요.

랑크

(헬머에게 속삭인다) **반박하지 말게.**

HELMER.

[taking her in his arms]. The child shall have her way. But tomorrow night, after you have danced—

NORA.

Then you will be free. [The MAID appears in the doorway to the right.]

MAID.

Dinner is served, ma'am.

NORA.

We will have champagne, Helen.

MAID.

Very good, ma'am. [Exit.]

HELMER.

Hullo!—are we going to have a banquet?

NORA.

Yes, a champagne banquet until the small hours. [Calls out.] And a few macaroons, Helen—lots, just for once!

헬머

(팔로 노라를 안으며) 우리 아기 마음대로 하세요. 그러나 내일 밤에 당신이 춤추고 난 후…….

노라

그때는 당신 맘대로 하세요. (하녀가 오른쪽 문에서 나타난다)

하녀

저녁 준비됐습니다, 마님.

노라

샴페인 준비해 줘, 헬렌.

하녀

알겠습니다, 마님. (퇴장)

헬머

와! 우리 파티하는 건가?

노라

네, 새벽까지 샴페인 파티하는 거예요. (큰 소리로 부른다) 그리고 마카롱 조금, 아니 많이 가져와, 헬렌……. 한 번뿐이니까!

HELMER.

Come, come, don't be so wild and nervous. Be my own little skylark, as you used.

NORA.

Yes, dear, I will. But go in now and you too, Doctor Rank. Christine, you must help me to do up my hair.

RANK.

[whispers to HELMER as they go out]. I suppose there is nothing—she is not expecting anything?

HELMER.

Far from it, my dear fellow; it is simply nothing more than this childish nervousness I was telling you of. [They go into the right-hand room.]

NORA.

Well?

MRS LINDE.

Gone out of town.

헬머

자, 자, 너무 흥분하지 말고 긴장하지 마. 예전대로, 내 작은 종 달새가 돼야지.

노라

네, 여보, 그렇게요. 하지만 이제 안으로 들어가세요. 랑크 선생님도요. 크리스티네, 머리 손질하는 것 좀 도와줘.

랑크

(나가면서 헬머에게 속삭인다) 아무 일도 없어야 할 텐데……. 무슨 일이 있는 건 아니겠지?

헬머

전혀, 자네에게 말했듯이 단지 어린애처럼 조바심이 나서 그런 것뿐이야. (그들은 오른쪽 방으로 들어간다)

노라

어떻게 됐니?

린데 부인

마을을 떠났대.

NORA.

I could tell from your face.

MRS LINDE.

He is coming home tomorrow evening. I wrote a note for him.

NORA.

You should have let it alone; you must prevent nothing. After all, it is splendid to be waiting for a wonderful thing to happen.

MRS LINDE.

What is it that you are waiting for?

NORA.

Oh, you wouldn't understand. Go in to them, I will come in a moment. [Mrs Linde goes into the dining-room. NORA stands still for a little while, as if to compose herself. Then she looks at her watch.] Five o'clock. Seven hours until midnight; and then four-and-twenty hours until the next midnight. Then the Tarantella will be over. Twenty-four and seven? Thirty-one hours to live.

노라

네 얼굴 보고 알았어.

린데 부인

내일 저녁에 돌아온대. 쪽지를 남기고 왔어.

노라

그냥 내버려 뒀어야 했는데. 아무것도 방해해서는 안 되니까. 어쨌든 놀라운 일이 일어나기를 기다린다는 것은 즐거워.

린데 부인

기다리고 있는 일이 뭔데?

노라

아, 넌 이해하지 못할 거야. 저분들 쪽으로 들어가. 나도 곧 갈게. (린데 부인이 식당으로 들어간다. 노라는 마음을 가라앉히려는 듯 잠시 가만히 서 있다가 시계를 본다) 다섯 시네, 자정까지 일곱 시간 남았고 내일 밤 열두 시까지는 스물네 시간. 그러면 타란텔라 춤은 끝날 것이고. 스물네 시간하고 일곱 시간? 남은 시간은 서른한 시간이야.

HELMER.

[from the doorway on the right]. Where's my little skylark?

NORA.

[going to him with her arms outstretched]. Here she is!

헬머

(오른쪽 문 앞에서) 내 종달새 어디 있지?

노라

(두 팔을 벌리고 헬머에게 가며) 저 여기 있어요!

ACT III

[THE SAME SCENE.—The table has been placed in the middle of the stage, with chairs around it. A lamp is burning on the table. The door into the hall stands open. Dance music is heard in the room above. Mrs Linde is sitting at the table idly turning over the leaves of a book; she tries to read, but does not seem able to collect her thoughts. Every now and then she listens intently for a sound at the outer door.]

MRS LINDE.

[looking at her watch]. Not yet—and the time is nearly up. If only he does not—. [Listens again.] Ah, there he is. [Goes into the hall and opens the outer door carefully. Light footsteps are heard on the stairs. She whispers.] Come in. There is no one here.

KROGSTAD.

[in the doorway]. I found a note from you at home. What does this mean?

제3막

(같은 배경. 무대 중앙에 테이블이 놓여 있고 테이블 주위의 의자 몇 개가 놓여 있다. 테이블 위에 램프가 타오르고 있다. 현관으로 들어가는 문은 열려있다. 위층에서 무도회 음악이 들린다. 린데 부인은 테이블에 앉아 한가하게 책장을 넘긴다. 책을 읽으려고 하지만 집중이 되지 않는 듯이 보인다. 가끔 바깥쪽 문에서 나는 소리에 귀를 기울인다)

린데 부인

(시계를 보며) 아직도 오지 않네, 곧 끝날 시간인데. 만약 그가 오지 않는다면 (다시 귀를 기울인다) 아, 왔다. (현관으로 가서 바깥 문을 조심히 연다. 계단에서 희미한 발걸음 소리가 들린다. 린데 부인이 속삭인다) 들어오세요. 여기 아무도 없어요.

크로그스터

(출입문에서) 집에서 당신이 남긴 메모를 봤소. 대체 무슨 뜻이오?

MRS LINDE.

It is absolutely necessary that I should have a talk with you.

KROGSTAD.

Really? And is it absolutely necessary that it should be here?

MRS LINDE.

It is impossible where I live; there is no private entrance to my rooms. Come in; we are quite alone. The maid is asleep, and the Helmers are at the dance upstairs.

KROGSTAD.

[coming into the room]. Are the Helmers really at a dance tonight?

MRS LINDE.
Yes, why not?

KROGSTAD.
Certainly—why not?

린데 부인

당신께 꼭 드릴 말씀이 있어서요.

크로그스터

그래요? 그리고 꼭 여기서 얘기할 필요가 있나요?

린데 부인

제가 사는 데는 힘들어요. 방 쪽으로 출입문이 없거든요. 들어오세요. 우리만 있어요. 하녀는 잠들었고 헬머 부부는 위층 무도회에 있어요.

크로그스터

(방 안으로 들어오며) 헬머 부부가 오늘 밤 정말 춤을 추나요?

린데 부인

네, 왜 안 되나요?

크로그스터

물론, 안될 것도 없죠.

MRS LINDE.

Now, Nils, let us have a talk.

KROGSTAD.

Can we two have anything to talk about?

MRS LINDE.

We have a great deal to talk about.

KROGSTAD.

I shouldn't have thought so.

MRS LINDE.

No, you have never properly understood me.

KROGSTAD.

Was there anything else to understand except what was obvious to all the world—a heartless woman jilts a man when a more lucrative chance turns up?

MRS LINDE.

Do you believe I am as absolutely heartless as all that? And do you believe that I did it with a light heart?

린데 부인

자, 닐스, 우리 얘기 좀 해요.

크로그스터

우리 둘 사이에 무슨 할 얘기가 있습니까?

린데 부인

얘기할 게 많아요.

크로그스터

나는 그렇게까지 생각 안 했는데요.

린데 부인

아뇨, 당신이 저를 온전히 이해하지 못했어요.

크로그스터

매정한 여자는 돈 많은 상대가 나타나면 남자를 버리는 온 세상이 뻔히 알고 있는 얘기 말고 뭘 더 이해할 것이 있소?

린데 부인

저를 그런 매정한 사람으로 생각하시나요? 그리고 제가 그런 일을 홀가분한 마음으로 했다고 믿나요?

KROGSTAD.

Didn't you?

MRS LINDE.

Nils, did you really think that?

KROGSTAD.

If it were as you say, why did you write to me as you did at the time?

MRS LINDE.

I could do nothing else. As I had to break with you, it was my duty also to put an end to all that you felt for me.

KROGSTAD.

[wringing his hands]. So that was it. And all this—only for the sake of money!

MRS LINDE.

You must not forget that I had a helpless mother and two little brothers. We couldn't wait for you, Nils; your prospects seemed hopeless then.

크로그스터

그렇지 않았소?

린데 부인

닐스, 정말 그렇게 생각하셨어요?

크로그스터

당신의 말대로였다면 그때 왜 내게 그런 편지를 보냈소?

린데 부인

별다른 방법이 없었어요. 당신과 헤어져야 할 때 당신이 내게 느꼈던 모든 감정을 끝내는 것도 제 의무였으니까요.

크로그스터

(손을 꽉 쥐며) 그랬군요. 그리고 이 모든 것이 단지 돈 때문이었소!

린데 부인

제게는 의지할 곳 없는 어머니와 어린 두 남동생이 있었다는 것을 잊지 마세요. 우리는 당신을 기다릴 수 없었어요, 닐스. 그 당시엔 당신 장래도 불투명했으니까요.

KROGSTAD.

That may be so, but you had no right to throw me over for anyone else's sake.

MRS LINDE.

Indeed I don't know. Many a time did I ask myself if I had the right to do it.

KROGSTAD.

[more gently]. When I lost you, it was as if all the solid ground went from under my feet. Look at me now—I am a shipwrecked man clinging to a bit of wreckage.

MRS LINDE.

But help may be near.

KROGSTAD.

It was near; but then you came and stood in my way.

MRS LINDE.

Unintentionally, Nils. It was only today that I learned it was your place I was going to take in the Bank.

크로그스터

그럴지도 모르지만, 다른 사람들을 위해서 나를 버릴 권리는 없었소.

린데 부인

정말 모르겠어요. 그렇게 할 권리가 있었는지 저 자신에게 수없이 되물었어요.

크로그스터

(좀 더 차분하게) 당신을 잃자 마치 온 땅이 내 발밑에서 나가떨어지는 것 같았소. 지금 내 꼴을 보시오. 난파선 조각에 매달린 조난자와 다름없소.

린데 부인

하지만 도움이 가까이 있을지도 모르죠.

크로그스터

거의 근처에 있었지만, 그때 당신이 나타나 방해했소.

린데 부인

고의가 아니에요, 닐스. 당신 대신 제가 그 은행에 들어가게 된 것을 오늘에야 알았어요.

KROGSTAD.

I believe you, if you say so. But now that you know it, are you not going to give it up to me?

MRS LINDE.

No, because that would not benefit you in the least.

KROGSTAD.

Oh, benefit, benefit—I would have done it whether or no.

MRS LINDE.

I have learned to act prudently. Life, and hard, bitter necessity have taught me that.

KROGSTAD.

And life has taught me not to believe in fine speeches.

MRS LINDE.

Then life has taught you something very reasonable. But deeds you must believe in?

크로그스터

당신이 그렇게 말하니 믿겠소. 하지만 이제 알았으니, 나에게 그 자리를 양보하지 않을 거요?

린데 부인

그럴 순 없어요, 그건 당신에게 조금도 도움이 되지 않으니까요.

크로그스터

오, 도움이라, 도움……. 나라면 어떻게 됐든 물러날 텐데.

린데 부인

저는 신중하게 행동하게 한다는 것을 배웠어요. 인생과 힘들고 호된 가난이 그것을 제게 가르쳐주었죠.

크로그스터

인생은 나에게 남의 듣기 좋은 말을 믿지 말라고 가르쳐 주었소.

린데 부인

그렇다면 인생이 당신에게 아주 합당한 것을 가르쳐주었네요. 그러나 행동은 믿으시죠?

KROGSTAD.

What do you mean by that?

MRS LINDE.

You said you were like a shipwrecked man clinging to some wreckage.

KROGSTAD.

I had good reason to say so.

MRS LINDE.

Well, I am like a shipwrecked woman clinging to some wreckage—no one to mourn for, no one to care for.

KROGSTAD.

It was your own choice.

MRS LINDE.

There was no other choice—then.

KROGSTAD.

Well, what now?

크로그스터

그게 무슨 뜻이오?

린데 부인

당신은 난파선에 매달린 조난자와 같다고 말씀하셨지요.

크로그스터

그렇게 말할 충분한 이유가 있으니까요.

린데 부인

그렇다면 저 또한 난파선에 매달린 조난자예요. 슬퍼할 사람도, 돌봐 줄 사람도 없어요.

크로그스터

그건 당신의 선택이었소.

린데 부인

그때 다른 길이 없었어요.

크로그스터

흥, 그래서요?

MRS LINDE.

Nils, how would it be if we two shipwrecked people could join forces?

KROGSTAD.

What are you saying?

MRS LINDE.

Two on the same piece of wreckage would stand a better chance than each on their own.

KROGSTAD.

Christine I······.

MRS LINDE.

What do you suppose brought me to town?

KROGSTAD.

Do you mean that you gave me a thought?

린데 부인

닐스, 우리 조난된 사람끼리 힘을 합치면 어떨까요?

크로그스터

그게 무슨 말이오?

린데 부인

같은 난파선 조각에 둘이 있는 것이 각각 따로 떨어져 매달려 있는 것보다 훨씬 나을 수 있어요.

크로그스터

크리스티네, 나는 ······.

린데 부인

제가 무엇 때문에 이 지역에 왔다고 생각하나요?

크로그스터

나를 생각했다는 말이오?

MRS LINDE.

I could not endure life without work. All my life, as long as I can remember, I have worked, and it has been my greatest and only pleasure. But now I am quite alone in the world—my life is so dreadfully empty and I feel so forsaken. There is not the least pleasure in working for one's self. Nils, give me someone and something to work for.

KROGSTAD.

I don't trust that. It is nothing but a woman's overstrained sense of generosity that prompts you to make such an offer of yourself.

MRS LINDE.

Have you ever noticed anything of the sort in me?

KROGSTAD.

Could you really do it? Tell me—do you know all about my past life?

MRS LINDE.

Yes.

린데 부인

저는 일하지 않고 살 수 없었어요. 제가 기억하는 한, 평생 일을 해 왔고, 또 일은 저의 가장 즐겁고 유일한 기쁨이었지요. 하지만 저는 지금 세상에 완전히 홀로 있어요. 인생이 너무나 공허하고 버림받은 느낌이에요. 저 자신만을 위해서 일하는 것에 조금도 즐거움이 없어요. 닐스, 제가 누군가를 위해서 일할 기회를 주세요.

크로그스터

믿을 수가 없소. 당신이 그런 제안을 하는 것은 여자의 감정에 휩쓸린 관대 의식일 뿐이오.

린데 부인

저에게서 그런 모습을 본 적이 있나요?

크로그스터

정말 그런 일을 할 수 있겠소? 말해 봐요. 내 과거의 일을 모두 아시오?

린데 부인

네.

KROGSTAD.

And do you know what they think of me here?

MRS LINDE.

You seemed to me to imply that with me you might have been quite another man.

KROGSTAD.

I am certain of it.

MRS LINDE.

Is it too late now?

KROGSTAD.

Christine, are you saying this deliberately? Yes, I am sure you are. I see it in your face. Have you really the courage, then—?

MRS LINDE.

I want to be a mother to someone, and your children need a mother. We two need each other. Nils, I have faith in your real character—I can dare anything together with you.

크로그스터

그리고 이 지역 사람들이 나를 어떻게 여기는지도 알고 있소?

린데 부인

당신은 저와 함께 있었다면 다른 사람이 되었을지도 모른다는 의미로 말씀하신 것 같은데요.

크로그스터

그건 확실하오.

린데 부인

지금이라도 너무 늦었나요?

크로그스터

크리스티네, 신중하게 말하는 거요? 맞아, 틀림없소. 당신 얼굴만 봐도 알 수 있지. 정말 그럴 용기가 있소?

린데 부인

저는 누군가의 어머니가 되고 싶어요. 그리고 당신 아이들도 어머니가 필요해요. 우리는 서로 필요해요. 닐스, 저는 당신의 진정한 성품을 믿어요. 당신과 함께라면 어떤 일도 해낼 수 있어요.

KROGSTAD.

[grasps her hands]. Thanks, thanks, Christine! Now I shall find a way to clear myself in the eyes of the world. Ah, but I forgot—

MRS LINDE.

[listening]. Hush! The Tarantella! Go, go!

KROGSTAD.

Why? What is it?

MRS LINDE.

Do you hear them up there? When that is over, we may expect them back.

KROGSTAD.

Yes, yes—I will go. But it is all no use. Of course you are not aware what steps I have taken in the matter of the Helmers.

MRS LINDE.

Yes, I know all about that.

크로그스터

(린데 부인의 손을 잡는다) 고맙소, 고마워, 크리스티네! 이제 세상 사람들 눈에 떳떳하게 보일 방법을 찾겠소. 아, 그런데 내가 깜박 잊고……

린데 부인

(귀를 기울이며) 쉿! 타란텔라 춤이 시작되었어요! 어서 가세요!

크로그스터

왜요? 무슨 일이죠?

린데 부인

저기 위층에서 춤추는 소리 들리죠? 그게 끝나면 사람들이 돌아올 거예요.

크로그스터

음, 그럼 돌아가겠소. 그런데 다 소용없게 됐군. 물론 당신은 내가 헬머가와 관련해서 어떤 조치를 했는지 모르겠지만 말이오.

린데 부인

아니오, 전 모두 알고 있어요.

KROGSTAD.

And in spite of that have you the courage to—?

MRS LINDE.

I understand very well to what lengths a man like you might be driven by despair.

KROGSTAD.

If I could only undo what I have done!

MRS LINDE.

You cannot. Your letter is lying in the letter-box now.

KROGSTAD.

Are you sure of that?

MRS LINDE.

Quite sure, but—

KROGSTAD.

[with a searching look at her]. Is that what it all means?—that you want to save your friend at any cost? Tell me frankly. Is that it?

크로그스터

그런데도 당신, 그럴 용기가 있단 말이오?

린데 부인

절망이 당신 같은 사람을 어디까지 끌고 가는지 저는 잘 알고 있어요.

크로그스터

내가 한 행동을 다시 되돌릴 수만 있다면!

린데 부인

할 수 없어요. 당신 편지는 지금 우편함에 들어 있어요.

크로그스터

확실하오?

린데 부인

확실해요, 하지만 …….

크로그스터

(린데 부인의 얼굴을 살피는 듯한 눈초리로) 그게 다 그런 뜻이오? 무슨 수를 써서라도 당신 친구를 구하려고 하는 것이죠? 솔직하게 말해 봐요. 그렇죠?

MRS LINDE.

Nils, a woman who has once sold herself for another's sake, doesn't do it a second time.

KROGSTAD.

I will ask for my letter back.

MRS LINDE.

No, no.

KROGSTAD.

Yes, of course I will. I will wait here until Helmer comes; I will tell him he must give me my letter back— that it only concerns my dismissal—that he is not to read it—

MRS LINDE.

No, Nils, you must not recall your letter.

KROGSTAD.

But, tell me, wasn't it for that very purpose that you asked me to meet you here?

린데 부인

닐스, 다른 사람을 위해서 자신을 희생한 여자는 두 번 다시 그런 일을 하지 않아요.

크로그스터

내 편지를 되돌려달라고 해야겠소.

린데 부인

아니에요, 하지 마세요.

크로그스터

아니오, 그렇게 할 거요. 헬머가 올 때까지 여기서 기다렸다가 내 편지를 돌려달라고 말하겠소. 그 편지는 단지 내 해고에 대한 것만 있으니 그걸 읽을 필요가 없다고 하겠소.

린데 부인

아니에요, 닐스, 당신은 편지를 회수해서는 안 돼요.

크로그스터

하지만, 당신이 여기서 나를 만나자고 한 게 바로 그 의도이지 않소?

MRS LINDE.

In my first moment of fright, it was. But twenty-four hours have elapsed since then, and in that time I have witnessed incredible things in this house. Helmer must know all about it. This unhappy secret must be disclosed; they must have a complete understanding between them, which is impossible with all this concealment and falsehood going on.

KROGSTAD.

Very well, if you will take the responsibility. But there is one thing I can do in any case, and I shall do it at once.

MRS LINDE.

[listening]. You must be quick and go! The dance is over; we are not safe a moment longer.

KROGSTAD.

I will wait for you below.

MRS LINDE.

Yes, do. You must see me back to my door.

린데 부인

처음에 놀랐을 때는 그랬어요. 하지만 그 후로 24시간이 지났고 이 집에서 믿을 수 없는 일들을 보게 되었지요. 헬머 씨는 그 일을 모두 알아야 해요. 이 불행한 비밀이 밝혀져 그들은 서로 완전하게 이해해야 합니다. 이 모든 것을 숨기고 거짓말을 계속하는 것은 불가능해요.

크로그스터

당신이 책임을 진다면 좋소. 하지만 어쨌든 내가 할 수 있는 일이 한 가지 있는데 즉시 하겠소.

린데 부인

(귀를 기울이며) 빨리 돌아가세요! 춤이 끝났어요. 더 있다가는 위험해요.

크로그스터

아래에서 기다리겠소.

린데 부인

네, 그래요. 집까지 바래다주셔야죠.

KROGSTAD.

I have never had such an amazing piece of good fortune in my life! [Goes out through the outer door. The door between the room and the hall remains open.]

MRS LINDE.

[tidying up the room and laying her hat and cloak ready]. What a difference! what a difference! Someone to work for and live for—a home to bring comfort into. That I will do, indeed. I wish they would be quick and come—[Listens.] Ah, there they are now. I must put on my things. [Takes up her hat and cloak. HELMER'S and NORA'S voices are heard outside; a key is turned, and HELMER brings NORA almost by force into the hall. She is in an Italian costume with a large black shawl around her; he is in evening dress, and a black domino which is flying open.]

NORA.

[hanging back in the doorway, and struggling with him]. No, no, no!—don't take me in. I want to go upstairs again; I don't want to leave so early.

크로그스터

내 인생에서 이렇게 놀라운 행운을 맞이한 적은 없소. (바깥문으로 나간다. 방과 현관 사이의 문이 열려있다)

린데 부인

(방을 치우고 모자와 외투를 챙겨 놓는다) 이렇게 달라지다니! 누군가를 위해 일하고 살아가는 안락한 가정. 내가 정말 그렇게 할 거야. 그들이 빨리 돌아왔으면 좋겠다. (귀를 기울인다) 아, 지금 오고 있군. 옷가지들을 입어야겠어. (모자와 외투를 든다. 헬머와 노라의 목소리가 밖에서 들린다. 열쇠가 꽂혀 돌아가고 헬머가 노라를 거의 강제로 현관으로 끌어들인다. 노라는 이탈리아 의상을 입고 커다란 검은 숄을 걸치고 있다. 헬머는 야회복을 입고 그 위에 앞이 트인 검은색 도미노를 걸치고 있다)

노라

(문 앞에서 머뭇거리며 남편과 실랑이를 벌인다) 싫어요, 싫다고요! 들여보내지 마세요. 다시 위층으로 가고 싶어요. 이렇게 빨리 떠나고 싶지 않아요.

HELMER.

But, my dearest Nora—

NORA.

Please, Torvald dear—please, please—only an hour more.

HELMER.

Not a single minute, my sweet Nora. You know that was our agreement. Come along into the room; you are catching cold standing there. [He brings her gently into the room, in spite of her resistance.]

MRS LINDE.

Good evening.

NORA.

Christine!

HELMER.

You here, so late, Mrs Linde?

헬머

하지만, 사랑하는 노라 …….

노라

제발, 토르발 …… 제발, 부탁이에요. 한 시간만 더 …….

헬머

일 분도 안 돼. 여보 노라, 우리 약속했잖아. 방으로 들어가. 거기 서 있으면 감기 걸려. (노라의 저항에도 불구하고 그녀를 방으로 점잖게 데려온다)

린데 부인

안녕하세요.

노라

크리스티네!

헬머

이렇게 늦게까지 여기 계셨군요, 린데 부인?

MRS LINDE.

Yes, you must excuse me; I was so anxious to see Nora in her dress.

NORA.

Have you been sitting here waiting for me?

MRS LINDE.

Yes, unfortunately I came too late, you had already gone upstairs; and I thought I couldn't go away again without having seen you.

HELMER.

[taking off NORA'S shawl]. Yes, take a good look at her. I think she is worth looking at. Isn't she charming, Mrs Linde?

MRS LINDE.

Yes, indeed she is.

린데 부인

네, 실례합니다. 드레스 입은 노라의 모습을 너무나 보고 싶어서
요.

노라

여기 앉아서 나를 기다리고 있었니?

린데 부인

응, 유감스럽게도 내가 너무 늦게 와서 네가 이미 위로 올라갔더
구나. 그래도 안 보고는 그냥 갈 수 없었어.

헬머

(노라의 숄을 걷으면서) **좋아요, 한번 보십시오. 봐 줄 만하지요.** 매
력적이지 않나요, 린데 부인?

린데 부인

네, 정말 예쁘네요.

HELMER.

Doesn't she look remarkably pretty? Everyone thought so at the dance. But she is terribly self-willed, this sweet little person. What are we to do with her? You will hardly believe that I had almost to bring her away by force.

NORA.

Torvald, you will repent not having let me stay, even if it were only for half an hour.

HELMER.

Listen to her, Mrs Linde! She had danced her Tarantella, and it had been a tremendous success, as it deserved—although possibly the performance was a trifle too realistic—a little more so, I mean, than was strictly compatible with the limitations of art. But never mind about that! The chief thing is, she had made a success— she had made a tremendous success. Do you think I was going to let her remain there after that, and spoil the effect? No, indeed! I took my charming little Capri maiden—my capricious little Capri maiden, I should say— on my arm; took one quick turn round the room;

헬머

눈에 띄게 예쁘지 않소? 춤출 때 다들 그렇게 생각했죠. 그런데 이 작고 귀여운 요정이 너무 고집을 부려요. 우리가 노라를 어떻게 해야 하죠? 제가 거의 강제적으로 데려왔다는 것을 믿기 어려울 거예요.

노라

토르발, 저를 30분 만이라도 머물게 하지 않은 것을 후회할 거예요.

헬머

듣고 있죠, 린데 부인! 노라는 타란텔라를 췄고 당연한 일이지만 정말 성공적이었습니다. 비록 그 춤은 예술의 한계와 엄밀히 조화를 이루는 것보다 조금 지나치게 사실주의적이긴 했지만 말입니다. 하지만 상관없어요! 중요한 건 노라가 이루어 냈죠. 꽤 성공적이었어요! 그 후에 제가 노라를 거기에 그냥 둬서 결과를 망쳤을 거라고 생각하나요? 절대, 아니죠! 나의 작고 소중한 카프리 소녀를 아니, 나의 변덕스러운 카프리 소녀라고 말해야겠네요. 내 팔로 안고 방을 한 바퀴 빠르게 돌면서

a curtsey on either side, and, as they say in novels, the beautiful apparition disappeared. An exit ought always to be effective, Mrs Linde; but that is what I cannot make Nora understand. Pooh! this room is hot. [Throws his domino on a chair, and opens the door of his room.] Hullo! it's all dark in here. Oh, of course—excuse me—. [He goes in, and lights some candles.]

NORA.

[in a hurried and breathless whisper]. Well?

MRS LINDE.

[in a low voice]. I have had a talk with him.

NORA.

Yes, and—

MRS LINDE.

Nora, you must tell your husband all about it.

NORA.

[in an expressionless voice]. I knew it.

모두에게 인사를 했죠. 그리고 소설에서 말하듯이 아름다운 환영은 사라져 버리는 거지요. 퇴장은 항상 인상적이어야 합니다, 린데 부인. 그런데 그것을 노라에게 이해시킬 수가 없죠. 아이고! 방이 덥네요. (도미노를 의자에 던지고 자신의 방문을 연다) **여기는 깜깜하네.** 응, 그럴 수밖에, 실례합니다 ……. (안에 들어가 촛불을 켠다)

노라

(서둘러 숨을 죽이고 속삭인다) **어떻게 됐니?**

린데 부인

(낮은 목소리로) 그 사람과 얘기했어.

노라

응, 그래서…….

린데 부인

노라, 네 남편에게 모두 털어놔야 해.

노라

(담담한 목소리로) 그럴 줄 알았어.

MRS LINDE.

You have nothing to be afraid of as far as Krogstad is concerned; but you must tell him.

NORA.

I won't tell him.

MRS LINDE.

Then the letter will.

NORA.

Thank you, Christine. Now I know what I must do. Hush—!

HELMER.

[coming in again]. Well, Mrs Linde, have you admired her?

MRS LINDE.

Yes, and now I will say goodnight.

HELMER.

What, already? Is this yours, this knitting?

린데 부인

크로그스터에 관해서 두려워할 필요가 없어. 하지만 남편에게 말해야 해.

노라

말하지 않을 거야.

린데 부인

그러면 편지가 알려 줄 거야.

노라

고마워, 크리스티네. 이제 내가 무엇을 해야 할지 알겠어. 쉿 ……!

헬머

(다시 나온다) 자, 린데 부인, 노라를 보고 감탄했나요?

린데 부인

물론이죠, 이제 그만 가봐야겠네요.

헬머

뭐라고요, 벌써? 이 뜨개질 거리, 부인 것입니까?

MRS LINDE.

[taking it]. Yes, thank you, I had very nearly forgotten it.

HELMER.

So you knit?

MRS LINDE.

Of course.

HELMER.

Do you know, you ought to embroider.

MRS LINDE.

Really? Why?

HELMER.

Yes, it's far more becoming. Let me show you. You hold the embroidery thus in your left hand, and use the needle with the right—like this—with a long, easy sweep. Do you see?

린데 부인

(집으며) 네, 감사해요, 깜빡 잊을 뻔했네요.

헬머

뜨개질하시나요?

린데 부인

그렇습니다.

헬머

자수를 하는 게 좋겠소.

린데 부인

정말요? 왜죠?

헬머

그게 훨씬 더 어울리니까요. 보여드리죠. 왼손으로 이렇게 자수를 잡고 오른손으로 바늘을 이용해서 길고 쉽게 곡선을 그리듯이 말이죠. 아시겠죠?

MRS LINDE.

Yes, perhaps—

HELMER.

But in the case of knitting—that can never be anything but ungraceful; look here—the arms close together, the knitting-needles going up and down—it has a sort of Chinese effect—. That was really excellent champagne they gave us.

MRS LINDE.

Well,—goodnight, Nora, and don't be self-willed any more.

HELMER.

That's right, Mrs Linde.

MRS LINDE.

Goodnight, Mr. Helmer.

린데 부인

네, 아마도…….

헬머

하지만 뜨개질은 결코 우아할 수가 없어요. 여기 보세요, 팔이 서로 맞닿아서 뜨개질바늘이 올라갔다 내려갔다 마치 중국인 같아요. 그나저나 그들이 우리에게 준 샴페인은 정말 좋았죠.

린데 부인

그럼, 안녕, 노라. 더 이상 고집부리지 말고.

헬머

옳은 말씀 하셨소, 린데 부인.

린데 부인

안녕히 계세요, 헬머 은행장님.

HELMER.

[accompanying her to the door]. Goodnight, goodnight. I hope you will get home all right. I should be very happy to—but you haven't any great distance to go. Goodnight, goodnight. [She goes out; he shuts the door after her, and comes in again.] Ah!—at last we have got rid of her. She is a frightful bore, that woman.

NORA.

Aren't you very tired, Torvald?

HELMER.

No, not in the least.

NORA.

Nor sleepy?

HELMER.

Not a bit. On the contrary, I feel extraordinarily lively. And you?—you really look both tired and sleepy.

NORA.

Yes, I am very tired. I want to go to sleep at once.

헬머

(문 있는 곳까지 따라가며) **안녕히 가세요, 댁에 편안히 가시길 바**
랍니다. 바래다 드리고 싶지만 여기서 그리 멀지 않으니, 잘 가시
오. (린데 부인이 나간다. 헬머는 따라간 후 문을 닫고 다시 들어온다) **아!**
드디어 쫓아냈어. 정말 지루한 여자야.

노라

몹시 피곤하지 않아요, 토르발?

헬머

아니, 전혀.

노라

졸리지는 않고요?

헬머

조금도 졸리지 않고 오히려 기운이 넘쳐. 당신은? 아주 피곤하고
졸려 보이는데.

노라

네, 정말 피곤해요. 바로 잠자리에 들고 싶어요.

HELMER.

There, you see it was quite right of me not to let you stay there any longer.

NORA.

Everything you do is quite right, Torvald.

HELMER.

[kissing her on the forehead]. Now my little skylark is speaking reasonably. Did you notice what good spirits Rank was in this evening?

NORA.

Really? Was he? I didn't speak to him at all.

HELMER.

And I very little, but I have not for a long time seen him in such good form. [Looks for a while at her and then goes nearer to her.] It is delightful to be at home by ourselves again, to be all alone with you—you fascinating, charming little darling!

헬머

거봐, 당신을 거기에 더 이상 머물지 않게 한 것이 옳았잖아.

노라

당신이 하는 건 모두 옳아요, 토르발.

헬머

(노라의 이마에 입을 맞추며) 이제야 내 종달새가 맞는 말을 하는군.
오늘 저녁에 랑크가 어찌나 기분이 좋았는지 당신도 봤어?

노라

정말요? 그분이요? 전혀 얘기도 못 했어요.

헬머

나도 거의 말 못 했지, 하지만 그 친구의 그렇게 기분 좋은 모습
을 오랫동안 본 적이 없어. (노라를 잠시 바라보고 가까이 다가간다)
다시 집에서 당신과 단둘이 함께 있으니 정말 좋군. 당신은 매력이
넘치고 사랑스러워!

NORA.

Don't look at me like that, Torvald.

HELMER.

Why shouldn't I look at my dearest treasure?—at all the beauty that is mine, all my very own?

NORA.

[going to the other side of the table]. You mustn't say things like that to me tonight.

HELMER.

[following her]. You have still got the Tarantella in your blood, I see. And it makes you more captivating than ever. Listen—the guests are beginning to go now. [In a lower voice.] Nora—soon the whole house will be quiet.

NORA.

Yes, I hope so.

노라

그렇게 바라보지 말아요, 토르발.

헬머

나의 가장 소중한 보물을 왜 내가 봐서는 안 되지? 어쨌든 미인은 내 것, 나만의 것인데?

노라

(테이블 반대편으로 가며) 오늘 밤엔 그런 식으로 말하지 말아요.

헬머

(노라를 따라가며) 보아하니, 당신 안에 타란텔라 춤의 열정이 아직도 남아 있어. 그래서 더 매력적으로 보이는 거야. 들어봐, 손님들이 이제 가기 시작해. (낮은 목소리로) 노라, 곧 집안 전체가 조용해질 거야.

노라

네, 저도 그랬으면 좋겠어요.

HELMER.

Yes, my own darling Nora. Do you know, when I am out at a party with you like this, why I speak so little to you, keep away from you, and only send a stolen glance in your direction now and then?—do you know why I do that? It is because I make believe to myself that we are secretly in love, and you are my secretly promised bride, and that no one suspects there is anything between us.

NORA.

Yes, yes—I know very well your thoughts are with me all the time.

HELMER.

And when we are leaving, and I am putting the shawl over your beautiful young shoulders—on your lovely neck —then I imagine that you are my young bride and that we have just come from the wedding, and I am bringing you for the first time into our home—to be alone with you for the first time—quite alone with my shy little darling! All this evening I have longed for nothing but you. When I watched the seductive figures of the Tarantella, my blood was on fire; I could endure it no longer, and that was why I brought you down so early—

헬머

그래, 내 사랑하는 노라. 당신과 함께 이런 파티에 나가도 내가
왜 말을 거의 하지 않고 멀리 떨어져서 가끔 당신을 몰래 훔쳐보
는지 알아? 내가 왜 그런 행동을 하는지 알겠어? 우리는 몰래 사
랑에 빠졌고 당신은 나의 비밀스러운 약혼자이며, 아무도 우리 둘
의 관계를 의심하지 않는다고 상상하기 때문이지.

노라

네, 항상 저를 생각하고 있다는 걸 잘 알고 있어요.

헬머

그리고 우리가 떠나면서 내가 당신의 아름답고 가녀린 어깨와 사
랑스러운 목에 숄을 걸쳐 줄 때 당신은 나의 어린 신부이고 우리
는 결혼식을 방금 마치고 돌아와서 처음으로 당신을 우리 집에 데
리고 간다고 상상하지. 당신과 단둘이 함께하기 위해, 수줍고 귀여
운 사랑하는 자기와 단둘이! 오늘 밤 내내 당신만 갈망했어. 타란
텔라 춤에서 유혹적인 모습을 보자 내 피가 끓어올랐지. 더 이상
참을 수가 없어서 당신을 빨리 데리고 왔던 거야.

NORA.

Go away, Torvald! You must let me go. I won't—

HELMER.

What's that? You're joking, my little Nora! You won't—
you won't? Am I not your husband—? [A knock is heard
at the outer door.]

NORA.

[starting]. Did you hear—?

HELMER.

[going into the hall]. Who is it?

RANK.

[outside]. It is I. May I come in for a moment?

HELMER.

[in a fretful whisper]. Oh, what does he want now?
[Aloud.] Wait a minute! [Unlocks the door.] Come, that's
kind of you not to pass by our door.

노라

저리 가세요, 토르발! 저를 놓아주세요. 저는 ·······.

헬머

뭐라고? 농담하는 거지, 내 귀여운 노라! 싫어, 싫다고? 나는 당신 남편 아닌가? (문밖에서 노크 소리가 들린다)

노라

(놀라며) 들었어요?

헬머

(현관으로 가며) 누구시오?

랑크

(밖에서) 나야, 잠깐 들어가도 돼?

헬머

(작은 소리로 투덜대며) 지금 시간에 뭘 원하는 거지? (큰소리로) 잠깐 기다리시게! (문을 연다) 들어와, 그냥 지나치지 않고 들러줘서 고마워.

RANK.

I thought I heard your voice, and felt as if I should like to look in. [With a swift glance round.] Ah, yes!—these dear familiar rooms. You are very happy and cosy in here, you two.

HELMER.

It seems to me that you looked after yourself pretty well upstairs too.

RANK.

Excellently. Why shouldn't I? Why shouldn't one enjoy everything in this world?—at any rate as much as one can, and as long as one can. The wine was capital—

HELMER.

Especially the champagne.

RANK.

So you noticed that too? It is almost incredible how much I managed to put away!

랑크

자네 목소리를 듣고 들러보고 싶은 생각이 들었지. (주위를 바르게 둘러본다) 아, 좋아! 사랑스럽고 편안한 방들이야. 당신들은 여기서 정말 행복하고 안락하게 살고 있지.

헬머

자네도 오늘 위층에서 꽤 유쾌해 보이던데.

랑크

무척이나. 왜 나라고 그래서는 안 돼? 왜 이 세상의 모든 것을 즐기면 안 되나? 어쨌든 할 수 있는 한 많이, 오래 즐겨야지. 그 와인 아주 훌륭했어…….

헬머

특히나 샴페인이 좋았어.

랑크

자네도 그렇게 생각했나? 얼마나 많이 마셔댔는지 거의 믿을 수가 없어.

NORA.

Torvald drank a great deal of champagne tonight too.

RANK.

Did he?

NORA.

Yes, and he is always in such good spirits afterwards.

RANK.

Well, why should one not enjoy a merry evening after a well-spent day?

HELMER.

Well spent? I am afraid I can't take credit for that.

RANK.

[clapping him on the back]. But I can, you know!

NORA.

Doctor Rank, you must have been occupied with some scientific investigation today.

노라

토르발도 오늘 밤 샴페인 많이 드셨어요.

랑크

그래요?

노라

네, 이이는 샴페인 마신 후엔 항상 이렇게 기분이 좋아요.

랑크

만족스러운 하루를 보낸 후에 유쾌한 저녁을 즐기지 말아야 할 이유가 없지?

헬머

만족스러운 하루? 유감스럽지만 그건 인정 못 하겠네.

랑크

(헬머의 등을 두드리며) 하지만 난 인정할 수 있다네!

노라

랑크 선생님, 오늘 과학적인 연구로 바쁘셨군요.

RANK.

Exactly.

HELMER.

Just listen!—little Nora talking about scientific investigations!

NORA.

And may I congratulate you on the result?

RANK.

Indeed you may.

NORA.

Was it favourable, then?

RANK.

The best possible, for both doctor and patient— certainty.

NORA.

[quickly and searchingly]. Certainty?

랑크

그렇소.

헬머

아니! 귀여운 노라가 과학적 연구에 대해 말하다니!

노라

그럼, 제가 그 결과에 축하해 드려도 될까요?

랑크

물론이지요.

노라

결과가 좋았군요?

랑크

의사와 환자 모두에게 최선의 결과일 수 있어요. 확실하죠.

노라

(재빠르게 살피듯이) **확실하다고요?**

RANK.

Absolute certainty. So wasn't I entitled to make a merry evening of it after that?

NORA.

Yes, you certainly were, Doctor Rank.

HELMER.

I think so too, so long as you don't have to pay for it in the morning.

RANK.

Oh well, one can't have anything in this life without paying for it.

NORA.

Doctor Rank—are you fond of fancy-dress balls?

RANK.

Yes, if there is a fine lot of pretty costumes.

NORA.

Tell me—what shall we two wear at the next?

랑크

절대적으로 확실해요. 그러니까 그 후에 즐거운 저녁을 보낼 자격이 있지 않나요?

노라

네, 그렇고말고요. 랑크 선생님.

헬머

나도 그렇게 생각하네, 아침에 지장을 주지 않는 한 말이야.

랑크

글쎄, 인생에서는 대가 없이 어떤 것도 가질 수 없지.

노라

선생님은 가장무도회를 좋아하시나요?

랑크

그렇소, 멋진 의상들이 많이 있다면야.

노라

저기, 다음번엔 우리 어떤 의상을 입으면 좋을까요?

HELMER.

Little featherbrain!—are you thinking of the next already?

RANK.

We two? Yes, I can tell you. You shall go as a good fairy—

HELMER.

Yes, but what do you suggest as an appropriate costume for that?

RANK.

Let your wife go dressed just as she is in everyday life.

HELMER.

That was really very prettily turned. But can't you tell us what you will be?

RANK.

Yes, my dear friend, I have quite made up my mind about that.

헬머

철부지 같으니라고! 당신 벌써 다음 무도회 생각을 하는 거야?

랑크

우리라고요? 그럼, 말씀드리죠. 부인은 착한 요정으로 가장하고 가세요.

헬머

그럼, 거기에 어울리는 의상으로 무엇을 추천하나? 뭐가 좋을까?

랑크

자네 부인은 평소와 같이 입어도 돼.

헬머

정말 잘도 둘러대는군. 그런데 자네는 무엇으로 가장할지 말해줄 수 없나?

랑크

말해주지, 이봐 친구, 나는 이미 정했다네.

HELMER.

Well?

RANK.

At the next fancy-dress ball I shall be invisible.

HELMER.

That's a good joke!

RANK.

There is a big black hat—have you never heard of hats that make you invisible? If you put one on, no one can see you.

HELMER.

[suppressing a smile]. Yes, you are quite right.

RANK.

But I am clean forgetting what I came for. Helmer, give me a cigar—one of the dark Havanas.

HELMER.

With the greatest pleasure. [Offers him his case.]

헬머

그래?

랑크

다음 가장무도회에서는 난 보이지 않을 거야.

헬머

재미있는 농담이야!

랑크

크고 검은 모자가 있는데 안 보이게 하는 모자라고 들어본 적 없어? 만약 자네가 그 모자를 쓴다면 누구도 자네를 볼 수 없지.

헬머

(웃음을 참으며) 그래, 그렇겠지.

랑크

여기에 왜 왔는지 깜빡했네. 헬머, 담배 하나 주게, 블랙 아바나로 말이야.

헬머

물론이지 (담배 상자를 내민다)

RANK.

[takes a cigar and cuts off the end]. Thanks.

NORA.

[striking a match]. Let me give you a light.

RANK.

Thank you. [She holds the match for him to light his cigar.] And now goodbye!

HELMER.

Goodbye, goodbye, dear old man!

NORA.

Sleep well, Doctor Rank.

RANK.

Thank you for that wish.

NORA.

Wish me the same.

랑크

(담배 하나를 꺼내 끝을 자른다) 고맙네.

노라

(성냥을 그으며) 불을 붙여드릴게요.

랑크

고마워요. (그가 담배에 불을 붙일 수 있도록 노라는 성냥을 들고 있다)
그럼, 안녕히들 계시오!

헬머

잘 가게, 친구!

노라

편히 주무세요, 랑크 선생님.

랑크

생각해 줘서 고맙소.

노라

제게도 인사해 주세요.

RANK.

You? Well, if you want me to sleep well! And thanks for the light. [He nods to them both and goes out.]

HELMER.

[in a subdued voice]. He has drunk more than he ought.

NORA.

[absently]. Maybe. [HELMER takes a bunch of keys out of his pocket and goes into the hall.] Torvald! what are you going to do there?

HELMER.

Emptying the letter-box; it is quite full; there will be no room to put the newspaper in tomorrow morning.

NORA.

Are you going to work tonight?

HELMER.

You know quite well I'm not. What is this? Someone has been at the lock.

랑크

부인에게도요? 좋소, 제가 잠을 푹 자기를 바란다면! 그리고 담 뱃불 고맙소. (두 사람에게 고개를 끄덕여 인사하고 나간다.)

헬머

(낮은 목소리로) 술을 많이 마셨군.

노라

(멍하니) 아마도요. (헬머는 주머니에서 열쇠 꾸러미를 꺼내 현관으로 간다) 토르발! 거기서 뭐 하시려고요?

헬머

우편함 좀 비우려고, 너무 꽉 차서 말이지. 내일 아침 신문 들어갈 자리도 없겠어.

노라

오늘 밤에 일하실 거예요?

헬머

일 안 할 거라는 거 당신이 잘 알잖아. 이건 뭐지? 누가 자물통을 만졌군.

NORA.

At the lock—?

HELMER.

Yes, someone has. What can it mean? I should never have thought the maid—. Here is a broken hairpin. Nora, it is one of yours.

NORA.

[quickly]. Then it must have been the children—

HELMER.

Then you must get them out of those ways. There, at last I have got it open. [Takes out the contents of the letter-box, and calls to the kitchen.] Helen!—Helen, put out the light over the front door. [Goes back into the room and shuts the door into the hall. He holds out his hand full of letters.] Look at that—look what a heap of them there are. [Turning them over.] What on earth is that?

NORA.

[at the window]. The letter—No! Torvald, no!

노라

자물통을요?

헬머

응, 누군가. 이게 무슨 일이지? 하녀가 그랬을 리는 없고……. 여기 부러진 머리핀이 있네. 노라, 이건 당신 것인데.

노라

(재빠르게) 아이들이 그랬나 봐요.

헬머

그럼, 아이들이 그런 짓을 못 하게 당신이 지도해야 해. 어이구, 드디어 **열었다.** (우편물을 꺼내고 부엌을 향해 소리 지른다) **헬렌! 헬렌, 현관문에 불을 꺼줘.** (다시 방으로 들어가 거실로 들어가는 문을 닫는다. 손에 수북이 쌓인 편지를 내보인다) **봐봐, 편지 꾸러미 쌓은 거.** (우편물을 뒤집으며) **도대체 이건 뭐지?**

노라

(창가에서) 그 편지다……. 안 돼요! 토르발, 안 돼!

HELMER.

Two cards—of Rank's.

NORA.

Of Doctor Rank's?

HELMER.

[looking at them]. Doctor Rank. They were on the top.
He must have put them in when he went out.

NORA.

Is there anything written on them?

HELMER.

There is a black cross over the name. Look there—what
an uncomfortable idea! It looks as if he were announcing
his own death.

NORA.

It is just what he is doing.

HELMER.

What? Do you know anything about it? Has he said
anything to you?

헬머

명함이 두 장인데 랑크 명함이군.

노라

랑크 선생님 것이라고요?

헬머

(명함을 보며) 의사 랑크. 맨 위에 있어. 아까 나가면서 넣었나 보군.

노라

거기 뭐라고 적혀있나요?

헬머

이름 위로 검은 십자가가 그어져 있어. 여기 봐 ……. 기분이 이상하군! 마치 자기 죽음을 알리는 것처럼 보여.

노라

바로 그거예요.

헬머

뭐라고? 알고 있는 거 있어? 당신한테 무슨 말을 했지?

NORA.

Yes. He told me that when the cards came it would be his leave-taking from us. He means to shut himself up and die.

HELMER.

My poor old friend! Certainly I knew we should not have him very long with us. But so soon! And so he hides himself away like a wounded animal.

NORA.

If it has to happen, it is best it should be without a word—don't you think so, Torvald?

HELMER.

[walking up and down]. He had so grown into our lives. I can't think of him as having gone out of them. He, with his sufferings and his loneliness, was like a cloudy background to our sunlit happiness. Well, perhaps it is best so. For him, anyway. [Standing still.] And perhaps for us too, Nora. We two are thrown quite upon each other now. [Puts his arms round her.] My darling wife, I don't feel as if I could hold you tight enough.

노라

네, 선생님이 제게 말하길, 명함이 오면 우리에게 작별하는 거라고 했어요. 틀어박혀서 죽을 거라는 뜻으로 말이죠.

헬머

내 불쌍한 친구! 우리가 오랫동안 함께 할 수 없다는 것을 알긴 했지. 하지만 너무 빨라! 마치 상처 입은 짐승처럼 자신을 숨기는군.

노라

만약 일어날 일이라면 아무 말 없는 게 최선이죠. 그렇지 않나요, 토르발?

헬머

(이리저리 왔다 갔다 하며) 그 친구는 우리 생활에서 하나가 되었어. 그가 없는 삶은 생각할 수 없어. 랑크가 짊어진 고통과 외로움은 우리의 햇살 같은 행복에 마치 구름 낀 배경과 같았지. 음, 아마도 그게 최선이었을 거야. 어쨌든 그 친구에게 있어서 말이야. 그리고 어쩌면 우리도 그렇지, 노라. 이제 우리 둘만 있소. (노라를 껴안는다) 나의 사랑스러운 아내, 당신을 꼭 붙잡을 수 있을 것 같이 느껴지지 않아.

Do you know, Nora, I have often wished that you might be threatened by some great danger, so that I might risk my life's blood, and everything, for your sake.

NORA.

[disengages herself, and says firmly and decidedly]. Now you must read your letters, Torvald.

HELMER.

No, no; not tonight. I want to be with you, my darling wife.

NORA.

With the thought of your friend's death—

HELMER.

You are right, it has affected us both. Something ugly has come between us—the thought of the horrors of death. We must try and rid our minds of that. Until then —we will each go to our own room.

NORA.

[hanging on his neck]. Goodnight, Torvald—Goodnight!

노라, 나는 당신에게 큰 재앙이 닥쳐 위협을 받을 상황에 놓이면 당신을 위해 내 목숨과 모든 것을 걸기를 바랄 때가 종종 있어.

노라

(뿌리치며 단호하고 분명하게 말한다) 이제 당신 편지를 읽으세요, 토르발.

헬머

아냐, 아냐, 오늘 밤은 읽지 않을래. 사랑스러운 당신과 함께 있고 싶어.

노라

친구의 죽음을 생각하는데도요?

헬머

그렇군, 그건 우리 모두에게 충격적인 일이야. 흉한 일이 우리 사이에 끼어들었어. 죽음의 공포에 대한 생각 말이지. 그런 생각은 빨리 떨쳐버리도록 해야 해. 그때까지 우리 각자의 방으로 가도록 하지.

노라

(그의 목을 껴안으며) 잘 자요, 토르발!

HELMER.

[kissing her on the forehead]. Goodnight, my little singing-bird. Sleep sound, Nora. Now I will read my letters through. [He takes his letters and goes into his room, shutting the door after him.]

NORA.

[gropes distractedly about, seizes HELMER'S domino, throws it round her, while she says in quick, hoarse, spasmodic whispers]. Never to see him again. Never! Never! [Puts her shawl over her head.] Never to see my children again either—never again. Never! Never!—Ah! the icy, black water—the unfathomable depths—If only it were over! He has got it now—now he is reading it. Goodbye, Torvald and my children! [She is about to rush out through the hall, when HELMER opens his door hurriedly and stands with an open letter in his hand.]

HELMER.

Nora!

NORA.

Ah!—

헬머

(노라의 이마에 입을 맞추며) **편히 쉬어, 내 작은 종달새. 잘자, 노라. 이제 편지나 읽어 봐야겠어.** (편지를 들고 서재로 들어가 문을 닫는다)

노라

(정신없이 더듬거린다. 헬머의 도미노를 집어서 둘러 입으며 빠르고 쉰 목소리로 더듬더듬 속삭인다) **다시는 그를 보지 못해. 다시는!** (머리 위로 숄을 뒤집어쓴다) **내 아이들도 다시 못 봐. 절대로! 깊이를 알 수 없는 차갑고 어두운 물속……. 이미 끝난 일이라면 좋을 텐데! 지금 편지를 들고 있을 거야, 이제 읽고 있어. 안녕, 토르발 그리고 내 아이들!** (노라가 현관으로 막 나가려고 하자 토르발이 급히 문을 열고 개봉한 편지를 손에 든 채 서 있다)

헬머

노라!

노라

아아!

HELMER.

What is this? Do you know what is in this letter?

NORA.

Yes, I know. Let me go! Let me get out!

HELMER.

[holding her back]. Where are you going?

NORA.

[trying to get free]. You shan't save me, Torvald!

HELMER.

[reeling]. True? Is this true, that I read here? Horrible! No, no—it is impossible that it can be true.

NORA.

It is true. I have loved you above everything else in the world.

HELMER.

Oh, don't let us have any silly excuses.

헬머

이게 뭐지? 이 편지 내용 알고 있지?

노라

네, 알아요. 저를 가게 해주세요! 나가게 해줘요!

헬머

(노라를 막으며) 어딜 가려고?

노라

(뿌리치려고 하며) 당신은 날 구할 수 없어요, 토르발!

헬머

(비틀거리며) 사실이야? 내가 읽은 것이 사실이냐고? 끔찍해!
안 돼, 안 돼. 사실일 리가 없어.

노라

사실이에요. 저는 이 세상 무엇보다도 당신을 사랑했어요.

헬머

바보 같은 변명 늘어놓지 마!

NORA.

[taking a step towards him]. Torvald—!

HELMER.

Miserable creature—what have you done?

NORA.

Let me go. You shall not suffer for my sake. You shall not take it upon yourself.

HELMER.

No tragic airs, please. [Locks the hall door.] Here you shall stay and give me an explanation. Do you understand what you have done? Answer me! Do you understand what you have done?

NORA.

[looks steadily at him and says with a growing look of coldness in her face]. Yes, now I am beginning to understand thoroughly.

노라

(그에게 한발 다가서며) 토르발!

헬머

한심한 여자야, 무슨 일을 한 거야?

노라

가게 해주세요. 저 때문에 당신이 고통받아서는 안 돼요. 당신이 감당해서는 안 돼요.

헬머

비참한 척하지 마, 제발! (현관문을 잠근다) 여기서 내게 설명해 봐. 무슨 일을 했는지 알고 있지? 대답하라고! 무슨 짓 했어?

노라

(물끄러미 보며 차가운 표정으로 말한다) 네, 지금에서야 저도 완전히 알기 시작했어요.

HELMER.

[walking about the room]. What a horrible awakening! All these eight years—she who was my joy and pride—a hypocrite, a liar—worse, worse—a criminal! The unutterable ugliness of it all!—For shame! For shame! [NORA is silent and looks steadily at him. He stops in front of her.] I ought to have suspected that something of the sort would happen. I ought to have foreseen it. All your father's want of principle—be silent!—all your father's want of principle has come out in you. No religion, no morality, no sense of duty—. How I am punished for having winked at what he did! I did it for your sake, and this is how you repay me.

NORA.

Yes, that's just it.

HELMER.

Now you have destroyed all my happiness. You have ruined all my future. It is horrible to think of! I am in the power of an unscrupulous man; he can do what he likes with me, ask anything he likes of me, give me any orders he pleases—I dare not refuse. And I must sink to such miserable depths because of a thoughtless woman!

헬머

이런 끔찍한 일이! 8년 동안 내 기쁨이자 자랑이었던 여자가 위선자에다 거짓말쟁이며 심각한 범죄자였다니! 그 모든 것이 말할 수 없을 정도로 추악해! 이게 무슨 꼴이야! 창피한 줄 알아! (노라는 침묵하며 헬머를 바라보고 있다. 헬머가 노라 앞에 멈춰 선다) 이런 일이 일어나리라는 것을 알았어야 했어. 예상했어야 했어. 당신 아버지의 부주의한 본성…… 입 다물어! 그 부주의한 본성이 모두 당신에게서 드러났어. 종교도, 도덕성도, 의무감도 없지. 당신 아버지가 한 일에 눈감아준 대가로 내가 이런 벌을 받아야 한다니! 당신을 위해서 한 일이었고 당신은 내게 이런 식으로 되갚다니.

노라

네, 그 말 그대로예요.

헬머

이제 당신은 내 행복을 모두 파괴했어. 내 미래도 모두 망쳐놨어. 생각만 해도 끔찍해! 나는 파렴치한 인간 손아귀에 들고 말았어. 그놈은 나를 제멋대로 할 거야, 자신이 원하는 것은 무엇이든 내게 요구하고 명령하겠지, 나는 감히 거절도 못 하고 말이야. 생각 없는 여자 때문에 비참한 구렁텅이에 떨어져야 한다니!

NORA.

When I am out of the way, you will be free.

HELMER.

No fine speeches, please. Your father had always plenty of those ready, too. What good would it be to me if you were out of the way, as you say? Not the slightest. He can make the affair known everywhere; and if he does, I may be falsely suspected of having been a party to your criminal action. Very likely people will think I was behind it all—that it was I who prompted you! And I have to thank you for all this—you whom I have cherished during the whole of our married life. Do you understand now what it is you have done for me?

NORA.

[coldly and quietly]. Yes.

HELMER.

It is so incredible that I can't take it in. But we must come to some understanding. Take off that shawl. Take it off, I tell you. I must try and appease him some way or another. The matter must be hushed up at any cost.

노라

제가 사라지면 당신은 자유로워질 거예요.

헬머

꾸며대지 마. 당신 아버지도 항상 그런 말을 달고 계셨지. 당신이 말한 대로 만약 당신이 사라진다고 해도 나에게 무슨 소용이 있을까? 조금도 없어. 그는 이 사건을 사방팔방에 알릴 것이고 만약 그렇게 한다면 난 당신의 범죄 행위에 관여한 것으로 부당하게 의심받을 수도 있어. 사람들은 그 사건의 배후는 나라고 생각할 거야. 당신을 부추긴 사람도 나라고 생각하겠지! 이 모든 것은 우리 결혼 생활 동안 내가 소중히 여긴 당신 덕분이야. 이제 당신이 내게 무슨 짓을 했는지 알겠어?

노라

(차갑고 차분하게) 네.

헬머

도무지 믿기지 않아서 받아들일 수 없어. 하지만 우리는 합의해야 해. 숄을 벗어, 숄 벗으라니까! 어떻게든 그놈을 달래야 해. 그 일을 무슨 일이 있어도 덮어버려야 해.

And as for you and me, it must appear as if everything between us were just as before—but naturally only in the eyes of the world. You will still remain in my house, that is a matter of course. But I shall not allow you to bring up the children; I dare not trust them to you. To think that I should be obliged to say so to one whom I have loved so dearly, and whom I still—. No, that is all over. From this moment happiness is not the question; all that concerns us is to save the remains, the fragments, the appearance—

[A ring is heard at the front-door bell.]

HELMER.

[with a start]. What is that? So late! Can the worst—? Can he—? Hide yourself, Nora. Say you are ill.

[NORA stands motionless. HELMER goes and unlocks the hall door.]

MAID.

[half-dressed, comes to the door]. A letter for the mistress.

그리고 당신과 나에 대해서 말하자면 우리 사이의 모든 것이 예전과 같이 보여야 해. 그러나 당연히 세상 사람들 눈에만 그렇게 보일 뿐이야. 당신은 내 집에 계속 남아 있을 거야, 그건 당연한 일이니까. 하지만 얘들 양육은 허락하지 않겠어. 당신에게 아이들을 믿고 맡길 수 없어. 내가 그토록 사랑해 왔던, 그리고 지금도 사랑하는 사람에게 이런 말을 해야 한다니! 아니, 이제 모든 것이 끝났어. 이 순간부터 행복이 문제가 아니야. 우리가 신경 써야 할 모든 일은 잔해와 파편 그리고 겉치레를 구하는 것이지.

(현관문 초인종이 울린다)

헬머

(깜짝 놀라서) 뭐지? 이렇게 늦은 시간에! 가장 끔찍한 일이? 그 놈인가? 당신 숨어, 노라. 당신 아프다고 해.

(노라는 꼼짝하지 않고 서 있다. 헬머가 나가 거실 문을 연다)

하녀

(옷을 반쯤 걸친 채. 현관으로 간다) **마님께 온 편지예요.**

HELMER.

Give it to me. [Takes the letter, and shuts the door.] Yes, it is from him. You shall not have it; I will read it myself.

NORA.

Yes, read it.

HELMER.

[standing by the lamp]. I scarcely have the courage to do it. It may mean ruin for both of us. No, I must know. [Tears open the letter, runs his eye over a few lines, looks at a paper enclosed, and gives a shout of joy.] Nora! [She looks at him questioningly.] Nora!—No, I must read it once again—. Yes, it is true! I am saved! Nora, I am saved!

NORA.

And I?

헬머

내게 줘. (편지를 가지고 문을 닫는다) 음, 그가 보낸 편지군. 당신은 가져서는 안 돼. 내가 읽어 보겠어.

노라

네, 읽으세요.

헬머

(램프 옆에 서서) 편지를 볼 용기가 안 나. 이건 우리 둘에게 파멸일지도 모르지. 아니야, 난 알아야 해. (편지를 뜯어 몇 줄을 재빨리 훑어본다. 동봉된 서류를 보고는 기뻐서 소리친다) 노라! (노라는 의아한 듯이 그를 바라본다) 아냐, 다시 한번 읽어봐야지. 좋아, 사실이야! 난 살았어! 노라, 난 살았다고!

노라

저는요?

HELMER.

You too, of course; we are both saved, both you and I. Look, he sends you your bond back. He says he regrets and repents—that a happy change in his life—never mind what he says! We are saved, Nora! No one can do anything to you. Oh, Nora, Nora!—no, first I must destroy these hateful things. Let me see—. [Takes a look at the bond.] No, no, I won't look at it. The whole thing shall be nothing but a bad dream to me. [Tears up the bond and both letters, throws them all into the stove, and watches them burn.] There—now it doesn't exist any longer. He says that since Christmas Eve you—. These must have been three dreadful days for you, Nora.

NORA.

I have fought a hard fight these three days.

HELMER.

And suffered agonies, and seen no way out but—. No, we won't call any of the horrors to mind. We will only shout with joy, and keep saying, "It's all over! It's all over!" Listen to me, Nora. You don't seem to realise that it is all over. What is this?—such a cold, set face!

헬머

당신도 마찬가지야, 당신과 나 우리 둘 다 살았어. 여기 봐, 그가 당신의 차용증서를 돌려보냈어. 자신이 크게 후회하며 그의 인생에 행복한 변화가 있다고 쓰여 있어. 뭐라 말하든 상관없어! 우리는 살았어, 노라! 누구도 당신에게 무슨 짓을 할 수 없어. 오, 노라, 노라! 아니, 먼저 이 꼴 보기 싫은 것부터 없애야겠어. 어디 보자……. (차용증서를 든다) 아니야, 안 볼래. 모든 일이 내게 나쁜 꿈이었을 뿐이야. (차용증서와 편지 둘 다 찢고 난로 속에 넣어 타는 것을 지켜본다) 자, 이제 더 이상 존재하지 않아. 크리스마스이브부터라고 쓰여 있던데 당신에게 끔찍한 사흘이었을 거야, 노라.

노라

사흘 동안 너무나 괴로웠어요.

헬머

그리고 힘들어하면서 방법도 찾지 못했으니……. 아니, 더 이상 끔찍한 일은 떠올리지도 말아야지. 그저 기뻐서 소리치며 "이제 끝났다, 모두 끝났어!"라는 말만 하면 돼. 내 말 들어봐, 노라. 끝났다는 것이 실감이 나지 않은 모양이군. 뭐지? 그런 차갑고 단호한 표정은!

My poor little Nora, I quite understand; you don't feel as if you could believe that I have forgiven you. But it is true, Nora, I swear it; I have forgiven you everything. I know that what you did, you did out of love for me.

NORA.

That is true.

HELMER.

You have loved me as a wife ought to love her husband. Only you had not sufficient knowledge to judge of the means you used. But do you suppose you are any the less dear to me, because you don't understand how to act on your own responsibility? No, no; only lean on me; I will advise you and direct you. I should not be a man if this womanly helplessness did not just give you a double attractiveness in my eyes. You must not think anymore about the hard things I said in my first moment of consternation, when I thought everything was going to overwhelm me. I have forgiven you, Nora; I swear to you I have forgiven you.

나의 불쌍한 노라, 충분히 이해해. 내가 당신을 용서했다는 것이 믿기지 않은 것 같은데. 하지만 그건 사실이야, 노라, 맹세해. 난 당신의 모든 것을 용서해, 나를 사랑해서 한 일이라는 것을 알고 있어.

노라

그건 사실이에요.

헬머

아내가 남편을 사랑해야 하는 것처럼 당신은 나를 사랑해 주었지. 단지 당신이 사용한 방법을 판단할 충분한 지식이 없었을 뿐이야. 당신 자신의 책임을 어떻게 조치해야 할지 모른다고 해서 내가 당신을 덜 사랑할 것 같아? 아냐, 아냐! 내게 기대기만 해. 당신에게 조언하고 지도해 주겠어. 이런 여성스러운 무력함이 내 눈에 더 큰 매력으로 보이지 않는다면 난 남자라고 할 수 없지. 처음에 놀라서 내가 심하게 한 말들에 대해 더 이상 생각하지 마. 그때는 모든 것이 나를 완전히 뒤덮으려는 것 같았으니까. 난 당신을 용서했어, 노라. 당신을 용서했다고 맹세해.

NORA.

Thank you for your forgiveness. [She goes out through the door to the right.]

HELMER.

No, don't go—. [Looks in.] What are you doing in there?

NORA.

[from within]. Taking off my fancy dress.

HELMER.

[standing at the open door]. Yes, do. Try and calm yourself, and make your mind easy again, my frightened little singing-bird. Be at rest, and feel secure; I have broad wings to shelter you under. [Walks up and down by the door.] How warm and cosy our home is, Nora. Here is shelter for you; here I will protect you like a hunted dove that I have saved from a hawk's claws; I will bring peace to your poor beating heart. It will come, little by little, Nora, believe me. Tomorrow morning you will look upon it all quite differently; soon everything will be just as it was before.

노라

용서해 주셔서 고맙군요. (문을 지나 오른쪽으로 나간다)

헬머

안 돼, 가지 마. (안을 들여다본다) 당신 거기서 뭐 해?

노라

(안쪽에서) 가장복을 벗으려고요.

헬머

(열린 문에 서서) 오, 그래. 진정하고 다시 마음을 편히 가져야지, 겁먹은 귀여운 종달새. 안심하고 쉬어. 난 당신을 보호해 줄 넓은 날개가 있어. (문 주변에서 왔다 갔다 하면서) 우리 가정은 얼마나 따뜻하고 편안한지 몰라, 노라. 여기가 당신 은신처야. 매의 발톱에서 구해낸 비둘기같이 당신을 보호하겠어. 가녀리게 뛰고 있는 당신의 심장을 진정시키겠어. 조금씩 그렇게 될 거야. 노라, 나를 믿어. 내일 아침이면 모든 것이 다르게 보일 거야. 곧 모두 예전과 같이 될 거야.

Very soon you won't need me to assure you that I have forgiven you; you will yourself feel the certainty that I have done so. Can you suppose I should ever think of such a thing as repudiating you, or even reproaching you? You have no idea what a true man's heart is like, Nora. There is something so indescribably sweet and satisfying, to a man, in the knowledge that he has forgiven his wife—forgiven her freely, and with all his heart. It seems as if that had made her, as it were, doubly his own; he has given her a new life, so to speak; and she has in a way become both wife and child to him. So you shall be for me after this, my little scared, helpless darling. Have no anxiety about anything, Nora; only be frank and open with me, and I will serve as will and conscience both to you—. What is this? Not gone to bed? Have you changed your things?

NORA.

[in everyday dress]. Yes, Torvald, I have changed my things now.

HELMER.

But what for?—so late as this.

내가 당신을 용서했다는 것을 확신할 필요가 없게 되고 당신은 내가 용서했다는 것도 확실히 느끼게 될 거야. 당신을 내치거나 심지어 비난할 거라는 그런 생각을 어떻게 할 수 있지? 당신은 진정한 남자의 마음이 어떠한지 잘 모르고 있어, 노라. 남자가 아내를 용서하는 것, 너그럽게 진심으로 용서하는 것이 말할 수 없을 정도로 유쾌하고 만족스러운 일이지. 그건 두 가지 이유로 자신의 것이 된 것이나 마찬가지니까. 말하자면 아내에게 새로운 삶을 주는 것으로 아내는 그의 부인이자 동시에 자식이 되는 것이지. 그러니까 당신은 이 일로 내게 그런 존재가 되는 것이야. 나의 귀여운 겁쟁이 아기. 어떤 일도 걱정하지 마, 노라. 솔직하게 내게 털어놔, 그러면 당신에게 의지와 양심적인 역할을 할 거니까. 뭐야? 잠자리에 안 들 거야? 옷을 갈아입었어?

노라

(평상복 차림으로) 네, 토르발, 지금 평상복으로 갈아입었어요.

헬머

그런데 뭐 때문에? 이렇게 늦은 밤에.

445

NORA.

I shall not sleep tonight.

HELMER.

But, my dear Nora—

NORA.

[looking at her watch]. It is not so very late. Sit down here, Torvald. You and I have much to say to one another. [She sits down at one side of the table.]

HELMER.

Nora—what is this?—this cold, set face?

NORA.

Sit down. It will take some time; I have a lot to talk over with you.

HELMER.

[sits down at the opposite side of the table]. You alarm me, Nora!—and I don't understand you.

노라

오늘 밤은 잠자리에 들지 않을 거예요.

헬머

아니, 여보 노라 ······.

노라

(자신의 시계를 보며) 너무 늦은 것도 아니에요. 여기 앉아봐요, 토르발. 당신과 저는 서로 할 얘기가 많아요. (테이블 한쪽에 앉는다.)

헬머

노라, 무슨 일이야? 이렇게 차갑고 단호한 표정은?

노라

앉으세요. 시간이 좀 걸릴 거예요, 당신과 나눌 얘기가 많거든요.

헬머

(테이블 반대편에 앉는다) 나를 불안하게 하는 군, 노라! 당신을 이해할 수 없어.

NORA.

No, that is just it. You don't understand me, and I have never understood you either—before tonight. No, you mustn't interrupt me. You must simply listen to what I say. Torvald, this is a settling of accounts.

HELMER.

What do you mean by that?

NORA.

[after a short silence]. Isn't there one thing that strikes you as strange in our sitting here like this?

HELMER.

What is that?

NORA.

We have been married now eight years. Does it not occur to you that this is the first time we two, you and I, husband and wife, have had a serious conversation?

HELMER.

What do you mean by serious?

노라

네, 바로 그거예요. 당신은 저를 이해할 수 없고 저도 당신을 이해한 적이 없었죠. 오늘 밤 이전에는 말이죠. 저기, 이야기 중단하지 마세요. 제가 말하는 것을 듣기만 해주세요. 토르발, 이건 관계를 정리하는 거예요.

헬머

그게 무슨 뜻이지?

노라

(짧은 침묵 후에) 우리가 여기에 이렇게 앉아 있는 게 이상하다고 느껴지지 않나요?

헬머

뭐가 이상해?

노라

우리는 결혼한 지 8년이나 됐어요. 우리 둘, 당신과 나, 남편과 아내로 진지한 대화를 나눈 것은 이번이 처음이라는 생각이 들지 않나요?

헬머

진지한 대화라니 무슨 말이야?

NORA.

In all these eight years—longer than that—from the very beginning of our acquaintance, we have never exchanged a word on any serious subject.

HELMER.

Was it likely that I would be continually and forever telling you about worries that you could not help me to bear?

NORA.

I am not speaking about business matters. I say that we have never sat down in earnest together to try and get at the bottom of anything.

HELMER.

But, dearest Nora, would it have been any good to you?

NORA.

That is just it; you have never understood me. I have been greatly wronged, Torvald—first by papa and then by you.

노라

8년 동안, 서로 알기 시작한 때부터라면 그 이상이죠. 우리는 어떤 심각한 문제에 대해 서로 대화를 주고받은 적이 없어요.

헬머

당신이 나를 도와서 떠맡을 수도 없는 걱정거리를 당신에게 끊임없이 언제까지나 말할 것 같았어?

노라

저는 그런 일 문제에 대해 말하는 것이 아니에요. 어떤 일이든 우리가 함께 노력하고 원인을 파악하기 위해 진지하게 앉아서 말한 적이 없다는 말이에요.

헬머

하지만 노라, 그게 당신에게 무슨 소용이 있었을까?

노라

바로 그거예요, 당신은 저를 조금도 모르시는 거예요. 저는 매우 부당한 취급을 받아왔던 거예요, 토르발. 처음에는 아빠에게서 그 다음엔 당신에게서 말이죠.

HELMER.

What! By us two—by us two, who have loved you better than anyone else in the world?

NORA.

[shaking her head]. You have never loved me. You have only thought it pleasant to be in love with me.

HELMER.

Nora, what do I hear you saying?

NORA.

It is perfectly true, Torvald. When I was at home with papa, he told me his opinion about everything, and so I had the same opinions; and if I differed from him I concealed the fact, because he would not have liked it. He called me his doll-child, and he played with me just as I used to play with my dolls. And when I came to live with you—

HELMER.

What sort of an expression is that to use about our marriage?

헬머

뭐라고! 우리 두 사람이라고…… 세상에서 그 누구보다도 당신을 사랑한 두 사람이 말이야?

노라

(머리를 저으며) 당신들은 나를 사랑한 적 없어요. 나를 사랑하는 것을 즐겁다고 생각했을 뿐이에요.

헬머

노라, 그게 무슨 말이야?

노라

친정에서 아버지와 함께 지낼 때, 아버지는 모든 일에 자기 생각을 말씀하셨고 그래서 저도 같은 생각을 가졌어요. 만약 아버지와 다르게 생각했어도 그 사실을 숨겼죠. 아버지가 그런 걸 좋아하지 않았을 테니까요. 아버지는 저를 인형이라고 불렀고 제가 인형을 가지고 놀았던 것처럼 아버지도 저와 놀아주셨어요. 그러다가 당신과 함께 살게 되었고요.

헬머

우리 결혼 생활에 무슨 그런 표현을 쓰는 거야?

NORA.

[undisturbed]. I mean that I was simply transferred from papa's hands into yours. You arranged everything according to your own taste, and so I got the same tastes as you—or else I pretended to, I am really not quite sure which—I think sometimes the one and sometimes the other. When I look back on it, it seems to me as if I had been living here like a poor woman—just from hand to mouth. I have existed merely to perform tricks for you, Torvald. But you would have it so. You and papa have committed a great sin against me. It is your fault that I have made nothing of my life.

HELMER.

How unreasonable and how ungrateful you are, Nora! Have you not been happy here?

NORA.

No, I have never been happy. I thought I was, but it has never really been so.

HELMER.

Not—not happy!

노라

(동요하지 않고) 제가 아버지 손에서 당신으로 옮겨졌다는 뜻이에요. 당신은 모든 것을 당신 취향에 맞게 정했고 저 또한 당신과 같은 취향을 갖게 되었어요. 아니면 그런 척했는지도 몰라요, 어느 쪽인지 정말 잘 모르겠어요. 때로는 이렇게도 때로는 저렇게도 생각해요. 되돌아보니 제가 이 집에서 하루 벌어 하루 먹고사는 가난한 여자처럼 살아왔던 것 같아요. 당신을 위해 애교를 부리는 존재였던 거죠, 토르발. 하지만 당신은 그게 맘에 들었던 거예요. 당신과 아버지는 제게 큰 죄를 지은 거예요. 내 인생에서 아무것도 이루지 못한 것은 당신들 잘못이에요.

헬머

당신이 이렇게 분별력도 없고 은혜를 모르는 사람이었다니, 노라! 여기서 행복하지 않았다는 거야?

노라

네, 전혀 행복하지 않았어요. 행복한 줄 알았는데 실제로는 그렇지 않았어요.

헬머

행복하지 않았다고!

NORA.

No, only merry. And you have always been so kind to me. But our home has been nothing but a playroom. I have been your doll-wife, just as at home I was papa's doll-child; and here the children have been my dolls. I thought it great fun when you played with me, just as they thought it great fun when I played with them. That is what our marriage has been, Torvald.

HELMER.

There is some truth in what you say—exaggerated and strained as your view of it is. But for the future it shall be different. Playtime shall be over, and lesson-time shall begin.

NORA.

Whose lessons? Mine, or the children's?

HELMER.

Both yours and the children's, my darling Nora.

NORA.

Alas, Torvald, you are not the man to educate me into being a proper wife for you.

노라

네, 단지 즐거웠을 뿐이었어요. 당신은 저에게 늘 친절했고요. 하지만 우리 집은 그저 놀이터에 지나지 않았죠. 제가 친정에서 아버지에게 어린 인형이었던 것처럼 당신에게는 아내라는 인형이었고 여기서 아이들도 저의 인형이 되었어요. 제가 아이들과 놀아주면 아이들이 기뻐하는 것처럼 저도 당신이 놀아줄 때 몹시 즐겁다고 생각했어요. 그게 우리 결혼 생활이었어요, 토르발.

헬머

바라보는 시각이 다소 과장되고 꾸며낸 듯하지만 당신 말도 일리가 있어. 하지만 장차 달라질 거야. 노는 시기는 끝났고 배우는 시기가 시작될 테니까.

노라

누가 배우는 거죠? 저예요, 아니면 아이들인가요?

헬머

당신과 아이들 둘 다 그렇지, 노라.

노라

아아, 토르발, 당신은 저를 당신에게 어울리는 아내로 가르칠 만한 사람이 아니에요.

HELMER.

And you can say that!

NORA.

And I—how am I fitted to bring up the children?

HELMER.

Nora!

NORA.

Didn't you say so yourself a little while ago—that you dare not trust me to bring them up?

HELMER.

In a moment of anger! Why do you pay any heed to that?

NORA.

Indeed, you were perfectly right. I am not fit for the task. There is another task I must undertake first. I must try and educate myself—you are not the man to help me in that. I must do that for myself. And that is why I am going to leave you now.

헬머

당신이 그런 말을 하다니!

노라

그리고 저 역시 아이들을 기르는데 얼마나 자격이 있나요?

헬머

노라!

노라

당신이 조금 전에 그렇게 말하지 않았나요? 제게 아이들 양육을 믿고 맡길 수가 없다고.

헬머

화가 나서 그랬지! 그 말을 왜 마음에 두는 거야?

노라

사실이에요, 당신이 정말 옳았어요. 저는 그 일에 적합하지 않아요. 먼저 책임져야 할 일이 있어요. 저 자신을 교육하는 데 노력해야 해요. 당신은 그런 일에 저를 도와주실 만한 분이 아니죠. 스스로 해야 하죠. 그래서 지금 당신을 떠나려고 해요.

HELMER.

[springing up]. What do you say?

NORA.

I must stand quite alone, if I am to understand myself and everything about me. It is for that reason that I cannot remain with you any longer.

HELMER.

Nora, Nora!

NORA.

I am going away from here now, at once. I am sure Christine will take me in for the night—

HELMER.

You are out of your mind! I won't allow it! I forbid you!

NORA.

It is no use forbidding me anything any longer. I will take with me what belongs to myself. I will take nothing from you, either now or later.

헬머

(벌떡 일어서며) 뭐라고?

노라

저 자신과 저에 관한 모든 것을 알려면 홀로서기를 해야 해요. 더 이상 당신과 함께 있을 수 없는 것은 그런 이유 때문이에요.

헬머

노라, 노라!

노라

지금, 당장 여기서 떠나겠어요. 오늘 밤은 크리스티네가 저를 받아줄 거예요.

헬머

당신 미쳤어! 내가 허락하지 않아! 내가 막는다고!

노라

더 이상 어떤 것도 저를 막아봤자 소용없어요. 제 물건은 가지고 가겠어요. 당신에게서 어떤 것도 받지 않을 거예요. 지금도 그렇고 앞으로도요.

HELMER.

What sort of madness is this!

NORA.

Tomorrow I shall go home—I mean, to my old home. It will be easiest for me to find something to do there.

HELMER.

You blind, foolish woman!

NORA.

I must try and get some sense, Torvald.

HELMER.

To desert your home, your husband and your children! And you don't consider what people will say!

NORA.

I cannot consider that at all. I only know that it is necessary for me.

HELMER.

It's shocking. This is how you would neglect your most sacred duties.

헬머

이게 무슨 미친 짓이야!

노라

내일은 집에 가겠어요. 친정집으로요. 뭔가 할 일을 찾기에는 그곳이 가장 편할 것 같아요.

헬머

당신은 분별없고 어리석은 여자야!

노라

분별력을 갖도록 노력해야겠어요, 토르발.

헬머

당신은 가정도, 남편도, 아이들도 버리겠다는 거야! 사람들이 뭐라고 할지 생각도 안 해!

노라

그런 건 조금도 생각할 수 없어요. 단지 이렇게 하는 것이 내게 필요하다는 것만 알아요.

헬머

충격이야. 이렇게 해서 당신의 가장 신성한 의무를 저버리는군.

NORA.

What do you consider my most sacred duties?

HELMER.

Do I need to tell you that? Are they not your duties to your husband and your children?

NORA.

I have other duties just as sacred.

HELMER.

That you have not. What duties could those be?

NORA.

Duties to myself.

HELMER.

Before all else, you are a wife and a mother.

NORA.

I don't believe that any longer. I believe that before all else I am a reasonable human being, just as you are—or, at all events, that I must try and become one.

노라

저의 가장 신성한 의무가 뭐라고 생각하시나요?

헬머

그걸 당신에게 말해줘야 하나? 당신의 남편과 아이들에 대한 의무가 아닌가?

노라

제게는 그것만큼이나 신성한 의무가 더 있어요.

헬머

그런 건 당신에게 없어. 그 의무가 도대체 뭐야?

노라

저 자신에 대한 의무예요.

헬머

무엇보다도 먼저, 당신은 아내이자 아이들의 어머니야.

노라

더 이상 그런 것은 믿지 않아요. 우선 저는 당신과 마찬가지로 온전한 인간이에요. 아니라면 어쨌든 그런 사람이 되기 위해 노력해야 해요.

I know quite well, Torvald, that most people would think you right, and that views of that kind are to be found in books; but I can no longer content myself with what most people say, or with what is found in books. I must think over things for myself and get to understand them.

HELMER.

Can you not understand your place in your own home? Have you not a reliable guide in such matters as that?— have you no religion?

NORA.

I am afraid, Torvald, I do not exactly know what religion is.

HELMER.

What are you saying?

NORA.

I know nothing but what the clergyman said, when I went to be confirmed. He told us that religion was this, and that, and the other.

저도 잘 알아요, 토르발, 대부분 사람은 당신이 옳다고 생각할 것이고 그런 의견은 책에서도 찾아볼 수 있죠. 하지만 많은 사람들이 뭐라고 하든 책에 뭐라고 쓰여 있든 저는 저 자신에 대해 더 이상 만족할 수 없어요. 저는 스스로 생각하고 이해하도록 노력해야만 돼요.

헬머

가정에서 당신의 본분을 이해 못 해? 그런 문제에 있어서 의지할 만한 안내인이 없어? 종교도 없어?

노라

유감이지만, 종교가 무엇인지 정확히 모르겠네요, 토르발.

헬머

무슨 말을 하는 거지?

헬머

제가 세례를 받았을 때 목사님이 말씀하신 것만 알아요. 목사님은 종교란 이러저러한 것이라고 말씀하셨어요.

When I am away from all this, and am alone, I will look into that matter too. I will see if what the clergyman said is true, or at all events if it is true for me.

HELMER.

This is unheard of in a girl of your age! But if religion cannot lead you aright, let me try and awaken your conscience. I suppose you have some moral sense? Or— answer me—am I to think you have none?

NORA.

I assure you, Torvald, that is not an easy question to answer. I really don't know. The thing perplexes me altogether. I only know that you and I look at it in quite a different light. I am learning, too, that the law is quite another thing from what I supposed; but I find it impossible to convince myself that the law is right. According to it a woman has no right to spare her old dying father, or to save her husband's life. I can't believe that.

제가 이 모든 것에서 벗어나 혼자가 된다면 그 주제를 알아보겠어요. 목사님이 하신 말씀이 사실인지, 아니면 어쨌든 저에게 맞는 말인지 알고 싶어요.

헬머

이런 말은 당신 또래의 여자들에게서 들어 본 적이 없어! 하지만 종교가 당신을 올바르게 안내할 수 없다면 내가 당신의 양심을 깨우도록 하지. 당신에게 도덕성은 있겠지? 아니면, 대답해 봐. 그것도 없는 건 아니지?

노라

그건 대답하기 쉬운 질문이 아니네요. 토르발. 전 정말 모르겠어요. 너무 당혹스러워요. 제가 아는 건 이에 대해 당신과 제가 너무나 다른 사고방식으로 바라본다는 것이에요. 법이라는 것이 제가 생각하고 있었던 것과 다르다는 것도 깨달았어요. 법이 옳다고 확신하는 것이 이제는 불가능하다고 생각해요. 법에 따르면 여자는 늙어서 죽어가는 아버지를 돌볼 권리도, 남편의 생명을 구할 권리도 없어요. 그런 법을 믿을 수가 없어요.

HELMER.

You talk like a child. You don't understand the conditions of the world in which you live.

NORA.

No, I don't. But now I am going to try. I am going to see if I can make out who is right, the world or I.

HELMER.

You are ill, Nora; you are delirious; I almost think you are out of your mind.

NORA.

I have never felt my mind so clear and certain as tonight.

HELMER.

And is it with a clear and certain mind that you forsake your husband and your children?

NORA.

Yes, it is.

헬머

어린애같이 말하는군. 당신이 살고 있는 세상의 상황을 이해하지 못하고 있어.

노라

네, 모르겠어요. 하지만 이제 알려고 노력하겠어요. 세상인지 아니면 저인지, 누가 옳은지 알아내려고요.

헬머

당신은 병에 걸렸어, 노라. 제정신이 아니야. 정신이 나간 것 같아.

노라

오늘 밤처럼 정신이 맑고 뚜렷한 적은 처음이에요.

헬머

당신 남편과 아이들을 버리는 게 맑고 뚜렷한 정신이야?

노라

네, 맞아요.

HELMER.

Then there is only one possible explanation.

NORA.

What is that?

HELMER.

You do not love me anymore.

NORA.

No, that is just it.

HELMER.

Nora!—and you can say that?

NORA.

It gives me great pain, Torvald, for you have always been so kind to me, but I cannot help it. I do not love you any more.

HELMER.

[regaining his composure]. Is that a clear and certain conviction too?

헬머

그렇다면 할 수 있는 설명은 단 한 가지야.

노라

그게 뭐죠?

헬머

당신은 나를 더 이상 사랑하지 않아.

노라

네, 바로 그거예요.

헬머

노라! 그런 말을 하다니!

노라

그렇게 말하는 저도 괴로워요, 토르발, 당신은 늘 저에게 친절하게 대해주었지만, 저도 어쩔 수가 없네요. 당신을 더 이상 사랑하지 않아요.

헬머

(평정심을 되찾으며) 그것도 분명하고 틀림없이 확신해?

NORA.

Yes, absolutely clear and certain. That is the reason why I will not stay here any longer.

HELMER.

And can you tell me what I have done to forfeit your love?

NORA.

Yes, indeed I can. It was tonight, when the wonderful thing did not happen; then I saw you were not the man I had thought you were.

HELMER.

Explain yourself better. I don't understand you.

NORA.

I have waited so patiently for eight years; for, goodness knows, I knew very well that wonderful things don't happen every day. Then this horrible misfortune came upon me; and then I felt quite certain that the wonderful thing was going to happen at last.

노라

네, 아주 분명하고 확실해요. 여기 더 이상 머물러 있고 싶지 않은 이유예요.

헬머

그럼 내가 무엇 때문에 당신의 사랑을 잃었는지 말해 줄 수 있어?

노라

네, 말씀드릴 수 있어요. 오늘 밤, 기적 같은 일이 일어나지 않았을 때 당신은 내가 생각했던 사람이 아니라는 것을 깨달았어요.

헬머

좀 더 자세히 설명해 줘, 이해가 안 돼.

노라

저는 8년 동안 끈기 있게 기다렸어요. 기적은 날마다 일어나는 일이 아니라는 걸 잘 알기 때문이죠. 제게 이 끔찍한 불행이 닥치자 드디어 기적이 일어날 거라고 확신했어요.

When Krogstad's letter was lying out there, never for a moment did I imagine that you would consent to accept this man's conditions. I was so absolutely certain that you would say to him: Publish the thing to the whole world. And when that was done—

HELMER.

Yes, what then?—when I had exposed my wife to shame and disgrace?

NORA.

When that was done, I was so absolutely certain, you would come forward and take everything upon yourself, and say: I am the guilty one.

HELMER.

Nora—!

NORA.

You mean that I would never have accepted such a sacrifice on your part? No, of course not. But what would my assurances have been worth against yours? That was the wonderful thing which I hoped for and feared; and it was to prevent that, that I wanted to kill myself.

크로그스터 편지가 저기 놓여 있을 때 당신이 그 남자의 요구를 받아들일 거라고는 상상하지도 않았어요. 당신이 그 남자에게 '세상에 모두 공개하라'하고 말할 것으로 확신했어요. 그리고 그랬다면…….

헬머

그래, 그다음에 어떻게 된다는 거야? 내 아내를 수치와 치욕에 드러냈다면?

노라

그랬다면 당신이 앞으로 나와 모든 것을 스스로 떠맡고 '제가 죄인입니다'라고 말씀하실 줄로 확신했죠.

헬머

노라!

노라

당신의 그런 희생을 제가 절대 받아들이지 않았을 거라는 뜻이죠? 그래요, 물론 그랬을 거예요. 하지만 제가 아무리 뭐라고 해도 당신의 뜻을 거스를 만큼 얼마나 가치가 있었을까요? 제가 기대하면서 두려워했던 기적 같은 일이 바로 그것이었어요. 그리고 스스로 목숨을 끊으려고 한 것도 그런 일을 막기 위해서였죠.

HELMER.

I would gladly work night and day for you, Nora—bear sorrow and want for your sake. But no man would sacrifice his honour for the one he loves.

NORA.

It is a thing hundreds of thousands of women have done.

HELMER.

Oh, you think and talk like a heedless child.

NORA.

Maybe. But you neither think nor talk like the man I could bind myself to. As soon as your fear was over—and it was not fear for what threatened me, but for what might happen to you—when the whole thing was past, as far as you were concerned it was exactly as if nothing at all had happened. Exactly as before, I was your little skylark, your doll, which you would in future treat with doubly gentle care, because it was so brittle and fragile.

헬머

난 당신을 위해 밤낮으로 기꺼이 일할 수 있어, 노라. 당신을 위해서라면 고통과 가난을 참을 수 있어. 하지만 어떤 남자도 사랑하는 사람을 위해 자신의 명예를 희생하지는 않아.

노라

수천수백만의 여자들이 그런 일을 했어요.

헬머

아, 당신은 생각하고 말하는 것이 마치 철없는 어린애 같아.

노라

그럴지도 모르죠. 하지만 당신은 저 자신을 내맡길 수 있는 남자답게 생각하거나 말하지도 않네요. 그리고 저를 위협하는 두려움이 아닌 당신에게 닥쳐올 두려움이 끝나자마자 모든 것이 지나갔을 때, 당신은 마치 아무 일도 일어나지 않은 듯하셨지요. 예전과 똑같이 저는 다시 당신의 귀여운 종달새, 인형이었고 그것은 연약하고 부서지기 쉬워서 당신이 앞으로 더욱더 섬세하게 보살피겠다고 했어요.

[Getting up.] Torvald—it was then it dawned upon me that for eight years I had been living here with a strange man, and had borne him three children—. Oh, I can't bear to think of it! I could tear myself into little bits!

HELMER.

[sadly]. I see, I see. An abyss has opened between us— there is no denying it. But, Nora, would it not be possible to fill it up?

NORA.

As I am now, I am no wife for you.

HELMER.

I have it in me to become a different man.

NORA.

Perhaps—if your doll is taken away from you.

HELMER.

But to part!—to part from you! No, no, Nora, I can't understand that idea.

(일어서며) 토르발, 저는 8년 동안 이곳에서 낯선 남자와 살면서 그에게 세 아이를 낳아 주었다는 것을 깨달았어요. 그렇게 생각하니 참을 수가 없네요! 저 자신을 갈기갈기 찢어버릴 수 있다면!

헬머

(슬퍼하며) 알겠어. 우리 사이에 깊은 구렁이 벌어진 거야. 부정할 수 없지. 하지만 노라, 그 틈을 채울 수는 없을까?

노라

지금의 저로서는 당신 아내가 아니에요.

헬머

나는 내가 다른 사람이 될 수 있다고 생각하는데.

노라

그럴지도 모르죠, 인형이 당신에게서 벗어난다면요.

헬머

헤어지다니! 당신과 헤어지다니! 안 돼, 노라, 난 그런 생각을 이해할 수 없어.

NORA.

[going out to the right]. That makes it all the more certain that it must be done. [She comes back with her cloak and hat and a small bag which she puts on a chair by the table.]

HELMER.

Nora, Nora, not now! Wait until tomorrow.

NORA.

[putting on her cloak]. I cannot spend the night in a strange man's room.

HELMER.

But can't we live here like brother and sister—?

NORA.

[putting on her hat]. You know very well that would not last long. [Puts the shawl round her.] Goodbye, Torvald. I won't see the little ones. I know they are in better hands than mine. As I am now, I can be of no use to them.

노라

(오른쪽으로 나가며) 그렇게 해야 모든 게 더욱 확실해져요. (망토와 모자를 챙기고 테이블 옆 의자에 둔 작은 가방을 들고 돌아온다)

헬머

노라, 노라, 지금은 아니야! 내일까지 기다려.

노라

(외투를 입으며) 낯선 남자의 집에서 밤을 보낼 수 없어요.

헬머

하지만 우리 여기서 남매처럼 살 수는 없을까?

노라

(모자를 쓰며) 그런 식으로 오래 지낼 수 없다는 것을 당신이 잘 아시잖아요. (숄을 두른다) 안녕히 계세요, 토르발. 아이들은 안 볼래요. 아이들은 저보다 더 나은 사람들의 보살핌을 받고 있어요. 지금의 저로서는 아이들에게 전혀 도움이 안 돼요.

HELMER.

But some day, Nora—some day?

NORA.

How can I tell? I have no idea what is going to become of me.

HELMER.

But you are my wife, whatever becomes of you.

NORA.

Listen, Torvald. I have heard that when a wife deserts her husband's house, as I am doing now, he is legally freed from all obligations towards her. In any case, I set you free from all your obligations. You are not to feel yourself bound in the slightest way, any more than I shall. There must be perfect freedom on both sides. See, here is your ring back. Give me mine.

HELMER.

That too?

NORA.

That too.

헬머

하지만 앞으로는, 노라, 앞으로…….

노라

제가 어떻게 말할 수 있겠어요? 저도 제가 어떻게 될지도 모르는데요.

헬머

하지만 당신은 내 아내야, 당신이 어떻게 되든 간에.

노라

잘 들으세요, 토르발. 지금 제가 하듯이, 아내가 남편 집을 떠나게 되면, 남편은 아내에 대한 모든 의무로부터 법적으로 자유로워진다고 들었어요. 어쨌든 저는 당신을 모든 책임에서 벗어나게 해드려요. 당신은 조금도 구속당한다고 느끼지 않을 거예요, 저도 마찬가지고요. 둘 다 완전히 자유로워져야 해요. 자, 당신의 반지를 돌려드려요. 제 것도 돌려주세요.

헬머

그런 것까지도?

노라

그래요.

HELMER.

Here it is.

NORA.

That's right. Now it is all over. I have put the keys here. The maids know all about everything in the house —better than I do. Tomorrow, after I have left her, Christine will come here and pack up my own things that I brought with me from home. I will have them sent after me.

HELMER.

All over! All over!—Nora, shall you never think of me again?

NORA.

I know I shall often think of you, the children, and this house.

HELMER.

May I write to you, Nora?

NORA.

No—never. You must not do that.

헬머

여기 있어.

노라

됐어요. 이제 모든 것이 끝났어요. 여기에 열쇠를 놓을게요. 하녀
들이 저보다 집안일을 훨씬 잘 알아요. 내일, 제가 떠난 후에 크리
스티네가 와서 시집올 때 가져왔던 제 물건을 꾸릴 거예요. 저에게
물건들을 보내도록 할게요.

헬머

모두 다 끝났어! 모두! 노라, 나를 다시 생각하지 않을 거야?

노라

당신과 아이들, 그리고 이 집이 자주 생각날 거라는 것을 알아
요.

헬머

당신에게 편지해도 돼, 노라?

노라

아뇨, 절대로. 그런 짓 하지 마세요.

HELMER.

But at least let me send you—

NORA.

Nothing—nothing—

HELMER.

Let me help you if you are in want.

NORA.

No. I can receive nothing from a stranger.

HELMER.

Nora—can I never be anything more than a stranger to you?

NORA.

[taking her bag]. Ah, Torvald, the most wonderful thing of all would have to happen.

HELMER.

Tell me what that would be!

헬머

하지만 그래도 보내게 해줘…….

노라

아무것도 안 돼요.

헬머

힘들면 내가 도와줄게.

노라

아뇨, 남에게서 어떤 것도 받지 않겠어요.

헬머

노라, 나는 당신에게 타인 이상은 절대 될 수 없는 거야?

노라

(가방을 들며) 아, 토르발, 가장 놀라운 일이 일어나야만 할 거예요.

헬머

그게 뭔지 말해줘!

NORA.

Both you and I would have to be so changed that—. Oh, Torvald, I don't believe any longer in wonderful things happening.

HELMER.

But I will believe in it. Tell me! So changed that—?

NORA.

That our life together would be a real wedlock. Goodbye. [She goes out through the hall.]

HELMER.

[sinks down on a chair at the door and buries his face in his hands]. Nora! Nora! [Looks round, and rises.] Empty. She is gone. [A hope flashes across his mind.] The most wonderful thing of all—?

[The sound of a door shutting is heard from below.]

노라

당신과 나 모두 변해야 하겠지요. 오, 토르발, 저는 더 이상 기적이 일어날 거라고 믿지 않아요.

헬머

하지만 난 기적을 믿겠어, 말해줘! 아주 달라진다면?

노라

우리가 함께하는 삶이 진정한 결혼 생활이 될 거예요. 안녕히 계세요. (복도를 통해 나간다)

헬머

(문 앞의 의자에 털썩 앉아 손으로 얼굴을 감싼다) **노라! 노라!** (주위를 둘러보고 일어선다) **텅 비었어. 가버렸어.** (그의 마음속에 희망이 떠오른다) **가장 놀라운 일?**

(밑에서 문이 닫히는 소리가 들린다.)

뭔가에 홀린 듯 고전문학 희곡 『인형의 집』을 읽게 되었습니다. 그리고 번역해야겠다는 결심을 하게 되었고 번역하면서 이 책을 더욱더 꼼꼼하게 곱씹으며 읽을 수밖에 없었습니다. 그러다가 유튜브로 인형의 집 외국 드라마까지 찾아서 보았는데요, 드라마로 보니 배경 상황과 등장인물의 감정선까지 거의 흡수하듯이 빠져들었습니다.

과거 유럽에서 여성의 지위는 우리나라 조선 시대와 별반 다르지 않았다는 것을 알 수 있었고 그 시대 문화의 잔재는 현대 사회를 살아가는 지금도 생활 곳곳에 많이 남아 있는 듯합니다.

이 책을 읽고 번역하면서 저도 모르게 화가 불쑥불쑥 치솟기도 하고 노라에게 연민을 느끼기도 했는데요, 등장인물 '노라'는 남편의 사회적 지위와 경제적 능력에 기대어 안락한 생활을 누리지만, 남편에게 받는 대우와 남편의 비위를 맞추기 위해 춤추고 노래하는 등 애교를 연구하는 노라의 모습이 애처롭게 느껴졌습니다.

하지만 린데 부인의 등장으로 인해 상황은 조금씩 달라지기 시작합니다. 처음에는 린데 부인의 시기심으로 한 가정이 깨졌다고 생각했는데 두 번, 세 번 반복해서 읽다 보니 어쩌면 노라의 자아를 찾아가는데 린데 부인의 간섭은 필수였다는 생각이 듭니다.

그런데 자아를 찾겠다고 남편, 아이, 가정을 버리고 집을 나가는 노라의 행동은 그 당시 시대 상황으로 봤을 때 너무 충격적이라 1879년 이 작품이 처음 발표되자마자 커다란 논란을 불러일으키며 많은 비난을 받았다고 합니다. 당시 성스러운 것으로 여겨졌던 결혼 생활과 가정 내 여성의 역할을 뒤흔드는 불쏘시개와 같은 역할을 했기 때문입니다.

노라의 남편인 헬머는 아내가 자신 몰래 돈을 빌린 사실을 알고 노라에게 불같이 화내며 맹렬하게 비난합니다. 노라는 그제야 자신의 존재를 깨달았는데요, 그동안 남편에게 사랑받는 줄로 알았던 자기 모습이 실제로 인간으로서 존중받지 못하는, 마치 인형과 같은 존재였음을 깨닫게 됩니다. 이 부분의 대사를 읽으면서 제가 만약 노라였더라도 남편에게 오만 정이 떨어졌겠다는 생각이 듭니다.

이와 동시에 '내가 그런 말을 듣는다면 나는 어떻게 행동했을까?'를 생각하게 되었는데요, 신뢰가 깨진 관계를 자녀들 때문에, 그리고 남편의 경제적 능력에 의지하기 위해 계속 이어 나가는 것이 맞는지 아니면 노라처럼 박차고 나갈 수 있을지 아직 고민 중입니다.

이 이야기를 조금 더 확장하자면 직장 또한 그렇지 않을까요? 많은 직장인이 회사 시스템, 직장 상사, 동료, 업무 문제 등 갖은 스트레스를 겪고 있어도 참고 다니는 것은 돈과 사회적 지위 때문인 경우가 대부분입니다. 퇴사하고 싶지만, 막상 퇴사하고 나면 뭐 먹고 살아야 할지 막막하니까 부당한 대우에도 당당하게 말도 못하고 참고 다닙니다.

저의 이야기를 잠깐 하자면, 13년 다닌 직장을 퇴사하고 프리랜서로 전향한 이유는 회사라는 조직이 결국 사람을 조정, 통제한다는 것을 깨달았고 더 이상 조직 구성원이 되지 않기로 결심했기 때문입니다. 그 당시 직장 내에서 받는 스트레스가 극에 달해서 계속 나쁜 생각이 들어 이성적 판단이 점점 흐릿해짐을 감지했습니다.

이렇게 우물쭈물 머물러 있다가는 마지막 퇴사 시기를 놓치고 영원히 조직에 속박되어 살 수밖에 없을 거라는 생각이 들어 정말 도망치듯이 나왔습니다.

준비 없는 퇴사는 위험하다, 월급만큼 벌 수 있는 여건을 만들고 나와야 한다는 조언은 쉴 새 없이 들었지만, 사람이 계획대로 살아갈 수 없는 것이 인생입니다. 실전에 뛰어들지 않은 상태에서 바깥 세상이 무서워 계속 준비만 하고 뚜렷한 성과를 내지 못한 저의 모습이 부끄러웠습니다.

그러다가 무슨 용기가 났는지 13년만에 사직서를 제출했습니다. 아마도 그 용기는 지금 당장 퇴사하지 않으면 죽을 것 같은 상황과 '그래, 13년이나 참고 다녔으면 이제 됐다, 미련 없다, 퇴사하면 후회하겠지만 먼저 살고 보자'라는 생각이 더해져 나온 결과물이었던 것 같습니다. 그때의 상황과 노라의 상황을 비교하여 생각하게 되었는데, '어쩜 이렇게 비슷할까?' 하는 생각이 들었습니다. 직장에서 받는 부당한 대우를 견디지 못하고 준비 없이 막무가내로 퇴사했기 때문이죠. 그동안 애지중지하게 여겼던 경력, 연금, 사회적 지위가 다 쓸모없게 느껴지는 순간 모두 다 내팽개치고 나왔습니다.

후회하지 않았느냐고요? 네, 무척이나 후회했습니다. 인내했던 시간이 참 아깝게 느껴졌습니다. 입사 후, 한 달 만에 나와 맞지 않는다는 것을 직감하였지만 '처음이라 그런가 보다.' 하고 참고 다녔습니다. 그리고 취업 준비에 쓰인 매몰 비용과 직업에 대한 사회적 지위, 은행 대출금도 무시할 수 없었습니다.

하지만 다닐수록 뭔가 쎄한 느낌은 사라지지 않았고 점점 더 커져만 가더라고요. 내가 어떤 사람인지를 알지 못한 채 무조건 남들이 인정해 주는 직업을 선택하고 주변 상황에 타협했던 나 자신에게 너무나 화가 났습니다. 그동안 여러 차례 탈출(?)을 시도했지만, 현실적인 문제 앞에서 속수무책으로 주변 상황이 바뀌기만을 바랐습니다. 나에게 어울리지 않은 옷을 억지로 껴입고 꾸역꾸역 참고 다녔던 13년의 세월, 에너지가 너무나 아깝습니다. 일찍이 진로를 바꿨더라면 지금쯤 전문가가 되어 있었을 텐데 말입니다.

다시 본론으로 돌아와서, 가정도 하나의 작은 조직인데 한 여성이 결혼하게 되면 여성의 지위가 남편의 경제적 능력과 사회적 지위에 따라 달라진다는 것은 부정할 수 없는 현실입니다. 하지만 한 가정을 꾸리기에 앞서 가장 먼저 고려해야 할 부분으로 배우자 간의 의사소통과 서로에 대한 신뢰도가 있겠지만 이보다 자아 정체성과 정신적, 경제적 독립이 가장 중요하다는 것을 노라의 가출 사건을 통해서 깨달았습니다.

그리고 가장 가까운 관계인 배우자로부터 존중을 받지 못한다면 대체 누구에게 인간 대접을 받을 수 있을까요? 인간관계는 서로를 존중하는 마음이 없다면 아무리 가족이라도 깊고 진실한 관계를 기대하기 힘듭니다. 권위적인 가장이 남자일 수도 있고 여자일 수도 있습니다. 문제는 그 가장의 성별이 문제가 아니고 약한 자들에게 군림하지 않고 오히려 섬기려고 하는 인격을 갖춘 사람인지가 중요합니다.

헬머가 노라에게 무심코 내뱉었던 말들, '종달새, 인형, 다람쥐'라고 자주 부르는 애칭, 겉과 속이 다른 이중인격성을 보면서도 자신이 인형처럼 조정당하고 있다는 사실조차 모른 체, 그런 행위들을 자신에 대한 애정 표현이라고 생각한 노라를 보며 현대 사회를 살아가는 우리도 어쩌면 비슷한 상황에 놓여 있는 건 아닌지 깊이 생각하게 되었습니다.

노라의 가출 사건이 없었더라면 헬머는 절대 변하지 않을 거라고 생각합니다. 주변 인물들에게 철부지 어린애 같은 이미지로 보였던 노라의 모습을 생각할 때, 정말 상상할 수 없을 정도로 변해버린 노라의 단호한 태도를 보면서 독자가 충격을 받을 수밖에 없고 작가는 이 점을 반전 포인트로 잡은 것 같습니다.

이 책은 여성뿐만 아니라 남성들도 필독서로 읽어야 하지 않을까 하는 생각이 듭니다. 헬머나 노라의 역할이 여자 또는 남자일 수도 있기 때문입니다. 누군가가 나를 조정, 통제하는 사람이 가족 구성원일 수도 있고 친구나 직장 동료일 수도 있습니다.

결혼 여부를 떠나서 우리 각자가 온전한 인격체로서 스스로 독립하여 자아 정체성을 찾는 것이 인생에서 가장 큰 숙제라는 생각이 듭니다.

독자 여러분의 진정한 자립을 기원하며
옮긴이 박정미

  인형의 집은 희곡 대화체로 이루어진 작품으로 영어원서와 영어 음성파일로 함께 공부한다면 언어 학습효과가 더욱 좋을 것입니다. 인형의 집 오디오북 음성파일은 유튜브에 있는 동영상 중에서 해당 파일을 공유하여 QR코드로 만든 것입니다. 저작권 문제로 MP3 파일 형식이 아닌 QR코드로 기재하오니 필요하신 분은 적극 활용하시기 바랍니다.

1. 스마트폰에 QR 앱 설치하기
2. QR 앱에 접속한 후 네모창이 뜨면 옆의 이미지 위로 QR코드 스캔하기

3. 링크 열기
4. 재생 버튼 누르기
※ 동영상 URL 주소
https://youtu.be/LgNN-6roFWw?si=ZRx-KtHYUcyatzfh

제이미북스잉 출간 서적

영어와 한글 함께 읽는 이솝 우화 시리즈

쓸수록 지혜로워지는 이솝우화 명언집
영작문 연습 & 영어 필기체 쓰기

읽을수록 지혜로워지고 영어실력이 향상되는
한영 요한복음/한영 잠언
내 영혼을 살리는 말씀 양식 112
신약성경 베스트 영어성경 말씀 암송 & 영어 필기체 쓰기